"Australia's biggest crime podcast is Ca[sefile ...] nameless host."

"Casefile: True Crime podcast becomes global hit."
Evening Standard

"As Casefile points out in their tagline, fact is scarier than fiction. But what the podcast might really prove is that fact is even scarier when told in a thick Australian accent – especially when accompanied by ambient, pulsing noise from a trio of professional sound designers and musicians."
Rolling Stone

"'Fact is scarier than fiction.' That's Casefile's tagline, and from the ominous sound effects to the anonymous host's voice, this Australian podcast really lives up to it."
Mental Floss

"Turning the volume way up yields a ghostly set of tinkling musical notes beneath the narration, adding a sinister layer to a production that already seems to echo from the depths of an old evidence locker."
A.V. Club

"Presented by an anonymous Australian presenter, Casefile is a true crime podcast that will prove fact is scarier than fiction."
Stay At Home Mum

HOW TO START A
PODCAST

Practical tips from the producer of
Casefile: True Crime Podcast

(2nd edition)

MIKE MIGAS

Copyright © 2020 Mike Migas LTD

All rights reserved. This book or any portion thereof may not be reproduced or used in any manner whatsoever without the express written permission of the publisher, except for the use of brief quotations in a book review.

For permissions contact:
www.mikemigas.com

Trade paperback ISBN:
9781549863059

Book formatting and cover design by:
Paulina Szymanska

Edit and proofread by:
New Generation Publishing

Disclaimer

The views and opinions expressed in this book are those of the author and do not necessarily reflect the views or positions of Casefile: True Crime Podcast and Casefile: True Crime Podcast team members.

CONTENTS

Introduction	ix
PART I	1
What is Casefile	3
Beginning	6
PART II – *Starting a Podcast*	15
Why Podcasting	20
Idea	27
Getting Started	36
First Episode	46
Recording Equipment	52
Recording Basics	67
Editing, Mixing and Mastering	76
Hosting	93
Artwork Design	100
Social Media, Website and Newsletter	109
Marketing	116
PART III – *Money*	127
Sponsorship	131
Affiliations	143
Store	148
Donations	155
Paywall	160
PART IV – *Growing Your Podcast*	165
Offers	168
Legal	174
Responsibility	178
The End	183
About the Author	186
Index	188

INTRODUCTION

Since early childhood, I loved to read. Some can say I was a real example of a bookworm; I tell them I like to get lost in a good story. Writing and reading often come in pairs, at least for authors. By any means, I wouldn't call myself one, but I developed an interest in writing since—as you might have guessed—early childhood.

During my teenage years, I started a school newspaper; I wrote articles, jokes, reviews. I drafted short stories and adventures for my tabletop gaming group. With time my interests switched to music, and after graduating from a music school for piano, I picked up a guitar. I still read a lot, but writing music was my new obsession.

Fast forward quite a few years. I graduated from university in the UK and found a job in my profession. I started writing articles for a potential blog, even though I didn't have a website at that time. Putting words on paper comes easily for me. I noticed it throughout my studies, and the idea of writing something more substantial than an essay was always at the back of my mind. Writing a book was something I always wanted to do, but I never followed that path.

After emigrating to the UK, my writing skills suffered. I spoke fluent English but not at the prose-writing level. Every immigrant knows that once you combine two languages, you lose finesse in both. That was one barrier to break through; another one was to come up with an interesting idea for a book. Should I write a novel? A guide for immigrants? Something about working in the film industry?

I didn't know where to start, so I did what seemed like the best option—I abandoned the idea and moved on with my life.

Fast forward a couple of years again, and *Casefile* happened. After a year of hard work and learning about podcasting, the concept of writing a book was back on my mind. I knew it wouldn't be a novel, more like a guide for aspiring podcasters, but still, I knew it would be enough to start. *Casefile*'s story was interesting, and I thought it would be cool to share it with the world.

The real reason for writing was to not only prepare an 'all-in-one' manual for podcasters but to show that it is possible to reach the top of the charts without being an insider, without the backing of the leading production companies. Not only that, I wanted to show it is possible to make money doing podcasts, to build a business around it.

Last year, a whole new world opened up to me, and I knew I had to share it with fellow audio enthusiasts. The opportunities and the possibilities of making a career from something so weird and yet so simple were too good to pass.

The book is for both fans of *Casefile* who want to learn more about the production of the podcast, and eager podcasters who want to start a show but don't know how.

I am aware that there are many materials online but what I'm offering may present a different view on it all. A year ago I didn't know anything about podcasting; now I'm working on one of the most popular true crime podcasts in the world. Second, I have a background in sound, so I care about the quality of production.

This guide will offer advice on setting up your recording space, recording practices and equipment. I try to stay away from more 'technical' language; my goal is to present you with a 'pain-free' way of podcasting. I want to show you the weird story of how *Casefile* came to be and share tips based on what I have learnt so far.

I'm not saying that I'm an expert in podcasting, hardly so. Each week, as we release new episodes, I discover something new. I know a lot more than I did a year ago and I think the knowledge could be valuable to you.

I'll describe writing the first episode, setting up recording equipment, a few recording basics and some production tricks. You will learn what you need to release a show, where to find help, and how best to market your podcast.

Of course, I will also talk about money. I warn you that money should be the last thing on your mind as podcasting is not a stable business. However, it is possible to get some dollars out of it.

I'll finish with what happens when you hit it 'big time' and what kind of offers you can expect.

It will not be a 500 page-long manual. I will not go deep into topics like mixing or editing. You can find resources online that will help you once you get that far.

I want to show you what you will need to run a podcast: the costs, the setup, the business of podcasting. Multiple things will need your attention when you decide to start a podcast. Well, at least if you want to have a successful show.

I hope you will enjoy the book and not be too harsh on me—it's my first one.

Mike

NOVEMBER 2019 UPDATE

A lot has happened since I released the first edition of the book, but one thing remained the same. We are still publishing *Casefile* episodes to a worldwide audience and developing as a team.

However, because I've learnt a few things in the last couple of years, I've decided to update this book with the latest information.

At the end of each chapter, where I feel I can add something extra, I will include a November 2019 update and list new tips and tricks that I've picked up. I always try to improve the production aspect of the show but there are a few new aspects of the business side of *Casefile*.

The podcasting landscape has also changed; there are celebrities, YouTubers and movie stars that have entered the space and big companies are looking at podcasting as something to invest in. Is it the 'golden age'?

I'm not too sure, the more people listening, the better—however, it also means that it becomes harder and harder for independent podcasters to rise to the top of the charts without a large marketing budget. It is still too early to predict how the podcasting industry will look in a few years, but I can assure you that the journey will still be interesting.

PART I

WHAT IS CASEFILE

Casefile is a podcast, an internet audio show. If I was to explain it to my grandma, I'd say it's like an old fashion radio broadcast, similar to Orson Welles' *The War of the Worlds*,[1] but based on real events. The description is far from perfect, but my grandma has just started learning about Facebook[2] so give her a break.

Casefile is an audio show, based on true crime stories. Although 'based' may be the wrong way to describe it, as it's more of a presentation of the facts. 'Based on' would indicate that there are opinions, speculations or exaggerations. *Casefile* has none of that. It's a non-biased, dry, straight-up description of real events. *Casefile* doesn't draw conclusions or speculate: we leave that element of the story for the listener.

Casefile is—for the most parts—a one-man show. Anonymous Host narrates the podcast and presents the listeners with the chronological development of a case. From time to time an episode includes original recordings from archives as well as re-enactments with hired actors.

The latter is rare as we try to stay with the original material whenever we can, but sometimes—due to copyrights and other issues—we experiment with the format.

What makes *Casefile* interesting is the depth of the research and the way the Host presents the story. It plays almost like a movie, with an introduction of characters, the incident, aftermath and conclusion.

The podcast deals with true crime stories; therefore, showing respect to the victims and anyone involved is our top priority during the production of the show. We stay away from sensationalism and judgement. Human nature is not black and white, and we don't paint it like that. There is a cause for every action, and *Casefile* wants to bring awareness to the principle.

Another thing that adds to *Casefile*'s uniqueness is the production. I keep the sound of the narrator's voice as natural as possible, without unnecessary bells and whistles. There are no irrelevant sound effects or distractions; we tend to keep it simple.

Music plays a huge part in creating the atmosphere of *Casefile*. Two composers—Andrew[3] and I—write bespoke music for each episode, and it plays a similar role to a movie soundtrack. It creates the ambience of mystery and tension; it directs the listeners and builds an emotional connection between the audience and the narrator's voice. Music is one of the main pillars of the show.

There are other smaller aspects of the podcast that make *Casefile* whole: social media, promo videos, additional content, the community, to name a few. But at its core, *Casefile* is a small group of people who work together to bring true crime stories to thousands of listeners, almost every week. There is no glamour, no fame, no spotlight. Hard work, dedication and authenticity make *Casefile* an excellent podcast, nothing else.

Other achievements include climbing as high as number four on iTunes's top charts[4] and winning the iTunes *Best of 2016* badge. We've also been featured on the iTunes[5] home page and had quite a few blogs written about us, alongside a couple of interviews with the Host of the show.

We are still learning, we are still growing, and we are still making mistakes.

The numbers show that I'm not exaggerating and that it is possible to start from nothing and develop a huge following in a short period. I wouldn't say it's easy or repeatable, but there are a few lessons that we learnt along the way, and in the next few chapters I'd like to share them with you. It's good to learn from your mistakes, but it's better to learn from the mistakes of others.

Too often I find that authors offer a 'blueprint' to success, a '3-step' manual to independence, and it annoys me. The claims usually have no validation in real life; there is no proof that any of the presented strategies work.

After a year of working on podcasts, I realised the obscurity of the subject and that I could offer a kind of manual for beginners. I appreciate that there are materials online around podcasting, but there wasn't anything from someone who reached the top of the charts in such a short time.

I wanted to write a short podcasting manual about sound production, scripting and setting up a podcast. But, I didn't want to make a promise that you could achieve similar results to *Casefile* in the same period by following the guide. I wanted to create something helpful and authentic. In addition to the above, I wanted to validate everything I present to you.

Yes, I have a background in sound, and I have worked as the editor on movies, but when I started producing podcasts, I started from zero. Neither the Host nor I knew anything about the business of podcasting when we first got together, and most of our venture was good old trial and error. There were a lot of mistakes along the way.

I wish to show you what happened behind the curtains and what you need to start a successful show that attracts the attention of hundreds of thousands—sometimes even millions—of people.

Last of all, I needed to establish that there is no 'blueprint' for success. There is no one magic way you can follow and find the 'holy grail' of podcasting. It's all about work, dedication, teamwork, luck, sweat and tears.

There were so many days when we wanted to throw in the towel and leave it all behind, go back to normal lives. We still have those moments, and I'm sure there will be more in the future.

Somehow we persisted and stayed on, with one intention on our minds: to make the best show we could.

---

1 Orson Welles – The War of the Worlds
   (*https://archive.org/details/WarOfTheWorlds1938RadioBroadcast256kbps*)
2 Facebook (*https://www.facebook.com*)
3 Andrew Joslyn Music (*http://www.andrewjoslynmusic.com*)
4 iTunes charts (*http://www.itunescharts.net*)
5 iTunes (*https://www.apple.com/itunes*)

BEGINNING

I don't need to say that the Host is a somewhat elusive figure. I have worked with him for more than a year now; we exchange emails almost every day, and we have long discussions before making an important decision about the podcast. And yet, there is little I know about him.

I don't know where he lives (I know it's Australia), I don't know what his exact job is, I don't know his marital status. So yes, he is rather a private man. His persona reminds me of the *Calvin and Hobbes*[6] author, Bill Watterson.

The Host knows that his background and his personal life don't matter for *Casefile*. His intention is to create the best true crime podcast in the world, to present the stories the best way he can, to make it worthwhile for the listeners. The best way to do that is to take the ego out of it.

What drives him to do it every week? I don't know.

I know it's not fame, so it can't be for the apparent reason. I know it's not money, otherwise, he would have quit a long time ago. I can take a wild guess that it is an urge to create, to make something, to leave a mark, however small it is. To be able to say, 'This is what I'm doing, and I'm doing my best.'

How did it all start? From what I gathered, it all started with sports. Football to be exact. During a game on one lazy afternoon, the Host got himself injured. He cracked his knee and required surgery to put it all back together. Funnily enough, I too had knee surgery during my teens, so I knew what came after that—a few days at the hospital and a few months of rehabilitation at home. You can't move much, sitting can be a struggle too, and there aren't a lot of activities you can pursue during recovery. It sucks.

The Host was not a big fan of podcasts; he mentioned that he listens to Joe Rogan's *Joe Rogan Experience*[7] and Dan Carlin's *Hardcore History*,[8] but that's about it. No experience in podcasting, storytelling or voice acting, just a man with a lot of spare time on his hands.

Usually busy with work, the Host found himself stuck at home, with not much to do. Because of his injury, he couldn't exercise, and he didn't want to sit on the couch and watch TV all day. It was not his style.

He played the guitar a bit. However, it was hard to practice music with an injured leg. It's difficult to play the guitar while lying down on the bed.

It was during one of Rogan's episodes that Joe praised the podcasting medium. In his opinion, everyone should start a podcast, even if it's just for fun. This statement struck a chord with the Host. He had a lot of free time, so starting a podcast sounded like a fun time killer.

Of course, the Host had doubts ('What would I even talk about? I'm no Dan Carlin'), but he decided that it could be amusing to try it and a good way to spend the rest of his free time. He had a simple recording setup, which he'd used for recording music in the past. On the equipment side, he was set and ready. The big question was, 'what kind of podcast should I start?'

After listening to *Hardcore History*, the Host knew he wanted to do something along those lines, a podcast based on facts and deep research. He says he was never a big true crime fan, but I think he may be downplaying his interests. I mean, I too like a good crime story and yet I would never start a true crime show myself. There must have been something more there. Something about his past? His real identity? Who knows? For now, it's all speculation.

Before he started the podcast, he had just finished watching *Making a Murderer*[9] on Netflix, which ignited the idea of a true crime show. He watched Australian shows *Blue Murder*[10] and *Underbelly*[11] on Melbourne gangland killings. That led to books about the characters like Neddy Smith, Roger Rogerson, Sally-Ann Huckstepp and Michael Drury.

It was another crime show that played a role in a birth of *Casefile*. Before commencing his research, the Host listened to the most famous true crime podcast, *Serial*,[12] and few episodes of other popular shows, to make sure that what he had in mind wouldn't be a copy of others. Once he found out that his podcast could fill a gap in the market, he was ready to go.

What was first, the episode or the name? According to my investigation, the first thing to come was the idea for the *Wanda Beach Murders* episode. It is a well-known Australian case, often repeated on TV there. The Host heard about it, but always in passing, so he didn't know any details about the incident itself. It felt like a perfect way to start off the podcast.

The research consumed him for days and nights as he was recovering from the injury. Apart from reports and online articles, he managed to track down a rare book in a local library. The book, *Wanted: A Casebook of unsolved crimes of violence in Australia*[13] by Timothy Hall, was so rare that he couldn't take it away from the study. He spent hours in the quiet and dusty room, reading the material and writing the first script. He also paid for a membership, which allowed him to search archived newspaper articles from the 60s; he didn't want to leave any resource behind.

It was a massive undertaking and making a coherent structure from all the data turned out to be a difficult task. It took him almost three weeks to complete the script. The Host almost gave up the pen and the temptation to abandon the idea was with him the whole time. It seemed silly to do all that work, investigating, looking for clues, researching. And for what? A podcast?

The Host had never recorded his voice before, so he wasn't sure if he wanted to go through with it, but he was too invested. He was beyond the point of safe return. Worst-case scenario, he would never release it.

During the investigation, he was also trying to come up with a name for the show. While reading some of the materials on the Wanda Beach Murders, there was a line in the article: it said, 'the police casefile is now over'. The Host stopped reading, picked up his pen and wrote down – Casefile. Casefile True Crime Podcast.

Sometimes the simplest ideas are the best ones, and they hit you without warning.

After completing the script, it was time for recording. The Host was in luck. He was the proud owner of a simple Rode microphone and Apogee One audio interface.[14] He had purchased the equipment as a means of recording his guitar, but now it would serve a different purpose.

He read the script out loud a few times and commenced the session. Every mistake he made, he would go back and record the sentence again, and it took him a few hours to complete the narration. But it wasn't over yet, far from it. He needed theme music, graphics, background score and someone who would set it all up for him. He had no idea how to upload the podcast and make it available online, but it wasn't enough to stop him.

First came the intro and theme music. After scouting a few royalty-free websites, the Host came across something that would fit his vision. A flatline sound effect and a creepy, ominous musical theme. Both would stay with *Casefile* from then on. The intro sound effect would get an upgrade eventually, but the theme music remained in the original form.

Next on the list was the score to assist the narration. The Host did the music himself, he enjoyed it but knew that in the future he might need extra help with that. But he brushed off the idea. There won't be any future! A few episodes at most and then back to work, finally back to normal life.

To publish the podcast, set it all up, get the right hosting and submit the show to iTunes was too much for one person. Especially a person who has never done anything quite like that. However, thanks to the power of the internet, nothing was lost yet. The Host knew he needed guidance; he scouted a few freelancing websites for someone who could advise him on podcasting, and hired a helping hand.

The show was now live. It wasn't anything big, heck, it was quite amateurish, to say the least. The research and writing were the backbones of the podcast, but the production, visual aspect and online presence were lacking. For the Host, none of the above mattered, he was already working on his second episode. And so it went. A second, third, fourth case...

He kept going, having fun and creating something that kept him occupied for those slow weeks he was spending at home. Nothing was indicating that the show would carry on after the rehabilitation was over. How surprised he was when the emails started to pour in! One after another, messages from listeners who praised his narration and attention to details. People wanted more episodes and cases from the anonymous Host. There was no marketing, no push, no advertisement. It was just him and his injured knee.

The beauty and power of the internet showed its best side, but not all the feedback was good. There were complaints about the sound quality of the narration, music levels and production.

The Host was at a crossroads. The whole *Casefile* project was meant to be a distraction, something to keep him busy. He could leave it all behind; there was no need to spend more time and money on it.

On the other hand, here was something that he had created and people were enjoying; he had so many ideas on developing it into something more, something bigger. If he was to choose that path, he knew he needed help, and needed it fast.

Enter me.

A few weeks back I had left my job as a team leader in the sound department at a movie studio. I needed a change and wanted to venture out on my own, try a bit of freelancing, that sort of thing. I had spent the last three years editing dialogue for movies, and it got boring. It was time to shift onto something new.

After leaving my job, I started looking at freelancing websites for small projects that would pay the rent while I figured out the next step. Editing audiobooks and podcasts seemed like the perfect fit for my skills, so I focused on those kinds of jobs. I came across an advert for a podcast that required some production work, and I answered the call.

I have to admit that it didn't pay well. But, I wasn't only looking for quick cash: I also wanted to explore a few ventures and find an endeavour that would put me on a new direction.

There were quite a few applicants, but I must have had the best resume—or maybe the Host liked my profile photo, who knows? I agreed to help out on *Casefile* on a casual basis and, if the Host didn't like my work, no worries. We would shake hands—over the internet—and go our separate ways.

At this point, I had to set up my workstation again. The best thing about working at a movie studio was that I had access to state-of-the-art equipment, but now it was gone. It took me a bit of time to get everything working at home again, but I was ready to tackle the business.

Let's be honest. I did an okay job. It was better than other applicants, but I didn't spend too much time on the podcast. The rate was rather low, and I had a few other podcasts I was editing at that time, *Casefile* was just one of many. It wasn't love at first sight, or hearing.

When did it become more than just a project? I'm not too sure. I knew that the show was getting quite a few listens, but I wasn't aware of whether the numbers meant anything significant. I did the job I was asked to do. The Host must have liked it, and he kept sending new episodes my way.

Even though we live half the world apart, we have a similar way of thinking: blunt, straight to the point, no need for further pleasantries. Somehow it works; he does his part, and I do mine. We both understand the power of collaboration and the fact that one person can rarely do it all.

Was it fate?

Luck?

Destiny?

I could have skipped his ad, as it was much lower than my usual rate. He could have abandoned the podcast, as it was draining his savings. I could have stayed one month longer at my job and never started my journey into podcasting. Could have, should have, would have.

I believe in cause and effect. The ancient law of nature that every decision has consequences. If you call it luck, then so be it. I call it being at the right time and place with the right set of skills, and then working hard and putting in the effort.

One thing is for sure, without the drive that the Host had in the beginning, none of that would have happened. Somewhere deep down he knew that he might have stumbled upon something special. Such opportunities are rare, so it would have been silly to have given it up.

Casefile's origin story is inspiring to me because it is not special at all. It involves a person who had a bit of spare time on his hands and decided to create something and release it to the world. That's it. No hidden agenda, no big investors, no funny anecdotes.

The inspirational part is that each one of us has the same chances and opportunities to do something like that. No one predicted that within a year *Casefile* would be one of the most popular true crime podcasts on the internet, I don't think anyone could have. That's the beauty and the lesson of it. Don't make unnecessary assumptions, get up and create something of value.

We all have hidden talents and predispositions: you may love dancing, someone else loves writing, another person may have a knack for maths. The internet allows everyone to show off his or her talents and the unique skills that we have within us. Not everything will turn out to be the next big thing, but that's not the point. The point is to not look for permission or inspiration to start.

You just need to show up.

NOVEMBER 2019 UPDATE

Four years later and *Casefile* is going stronger than ever. We've assembled a team of unbelievably skilled and hardworking people and, even though we all work remotely, in a way the work for me is more meaningful than all of my previous jobs combined. We could also quit our jobs and focus on the show full-time.

The most recent change for us was to start *Casefile Presents*[15]—a platform that aims at producing and releasing stories that we find powerful and impactful. To dip our toe, we've started with a podcast called *From the Files*,[16] which is a companion show to *Casefile*. Released monthly, it updates the listeners on the latest developments from cases that we've previously featured on *Casefile*. Besides that, we also interview people connected to the incidents.

However, the first standalone show that released was called *Silent Waves*[17] and, even though it was a re-release on the platform, we felt that the honest and powerful story deserved a bigger audience. There are more shows in production, as well as many ideas, and only the future will tell us how this new venture will develop.

---

6 Calvin and Hobbes (*https://www.calvinandhobbes.com*)
7 Joe Rogan Experience (*http://podcasts.joerogan.net*)
8 Hardcore History (*https://www.dancarlin.com/hardcore-history-series*)
9 Making a Murderer (*https://www.netflix.com/gb/title/80000770*)
10 Blue Murder (*https://www.imdb.com/title/tt0364797*)
11 Underbelly (*https://www.imdb.com/title/tt1119176*)
12 Serial (*https://serialpodcast.org*)
13 Timothy Hall – Wanted: A Casebook of unsolved crimes of violence in Australia (*https://www.goodreads.com/book/show/3324357-wanted*)
14 Apogee One audio interface (*https://apogeedigital.com/products/one*)
15 Casefile Presents (*https://casefilepresents.com*)
16 From the Files (*https://fromthefiles.com*)
17 Silent Waves (*https://silentwavespodcast.com*)

PART II

Starting a Podcast

When I started to learn about internet marketing, blogging and affiliate marketing, I was sceptical at best. Not to mention the claims of people who were making a living by writing a blog or running a YouTube[18] channel. The adventure with *Casefile* changed my mind. Even though the podcast is still at its beginnings, it showed me what was possible. Now, I tell my family and friends to act on their ideas, to experiment, to just do it. It may or may not work, but there is a small chance that something amazing will happen.

What is the future of *Casefile*? I'm not sure. We are still learning, more than often, from our mistakes. The show may last for years, or maybe it will all fall apart in the next few months. One thing is crystal clear; I have my eyes opened now. I know what is possible and that, with hard work, dedication and luck, this kind of success is repeatable.

I won't be offering a 'blueprint' or 'three steps to success'. I don't think it is possible to have something like that. I believe that hard work and commitment will take you far, but you also need a bit of luck. It's just how it works.

It should not discourage you, though; every situation in life requires a bit of luck, but if you don't take a chance, you never find out if the good fortune will find you too. Remember that someone once said, "The harder I work, the luckier I get."

I don't need to say that by producing *Casefile* I learnt quite a bit about the business of podcasting. A lot from research and even more by doing the show. I wanted to create a practical manual based on my experiences, everything that I have learnt in one place.

I've split the rest of the book into three segments.

PART II—STARTING A PODCAST

Here you will learn everything you need to start your podcast. I will start with ideas for your show and how to come up with one, how to write your first episode and then how to record it.

I am an audio professional, so I will offer you a few thoughts on recording, a few basic tips and tricks. Editing and post-production are important, and I want to make you aware of how much work goes into each step—unfortunately, it is not as easy as 'plug and play'.

In the second part of the segment, I will talk about hosting your podcast and the costs of it, the artwork design, social media and marketing. It doesn't make much sense to spend all that time writing, recording and editing your show if you only play it to your family and friends.

PART III—MONEY

In this part, we will talk about money. I will say it now; if you are starting a podcast to become rich, then it's going to be a rough road. Not impossible, but really, really difficult.

It doesn't mean that you can't make money out of it, you can, and some people do. I will show you how monetising a podcast works and some ways of making money off your show. I'm not saying these are all the options, but these are the ways that I tested out with either *Casefile* or my other ventures.

I will talk about sponsorship and how it works (and why it isn't as simple as it sounds), affiliations, merchandise and donations. Each one of these avenues can make you extra cash and help support your podcast. Who knows? Maybe it will become your full-time job at some point... One thing is for sure, even with the level of success that is possible, many still have to keep other jobs to pay the bills.

PART IV—GROWING YOUR PODCAST

In the last and the shortest segment of the book, I want to discuss what happens when you hit large download numbers. It is awesome that so many people enjoy and listen to your work, but sure enough, there are additional costs and issues that will need attending.

    I will point out some of the offers you may get when you reach large download numbers. With advertising and affiliations come legal advice and other responsibilities in keeping the podcast thriving.

---

18 YouTube (https://www.youtube.com)

WHY PODCASTING

Podcasts are here to stay, at least for the foreseeable future. At the end of this chapter, I'll share statistics to strengthen this claim. First, let's try to answer a question: why is podcasting on the rise? Why is it a perfect medium to convey a message?

For me, it's about the stories and a little bit about history. Why history? Well, history likes to repeat itself. In the beginning, we had Gutenberg's printing press,[19] then the Industrial Revolution gave us the radio, then the TV, and then came the internet. With the internet, all of that came back in new, instant and direct form. YouTube[20] for videos, blogs and websites for press and now podcasts for radio.

Podcasts are, of course, nothing new. It's another medium that helps people to do what they do best, tell stories. Orson Welles' *The War of the Worlds*[21] from 1938 comes to mind, among other radio broadcasts that people listened to in the past.

I remember tuning into my grandpa's old radio, to talk shows, interviews, politics. He also used to play us children's stories on vinyl; we would often fall asleep to a slowly turning disc that—with occasional skips and scratches—would take us into another world. Podcasts are a natural evolution of that, but mobile, instantaneous and unlimited. I also find the medium quite intimate and personal.

With TV and movies, you can have more than just one person watching and listening, same with games or music, though music often offers personal escapism too.

When I learnt about podcasting, I immediately thought about books and how they work. When you read, it's just you and the author. The connection feels strong and real. As you are reading these words, it seems like I'm talking to you directly. Not to your friends or people on the train, just to you. It's the same with podcasts.

You put your headphones on and escape from thoughts, from the surrounding world. You can listen to podcasts during your work commute, at the gym or when you are walking a dog, but for some time it's just you and the host. You tune into what he or she has to say and listen to the stories.

There are many different kinds of podcasts; true crime shows like *Casefile*, talk shows, business shows, comedy shows. All play the same function: they tell stories, they carry a message.

Another element that adds to the intimacy of podcasting is the human voice. Human hearing range is between 20 Hz to 20 kHz,[22] but the part that we are most sensitive to is around 1 kHz–5 kHz.

Why is that important? That's the range of a human voice. People are sensitive to a human voice, and it's how we evolved. It helps with communication between people; it helps for the species to survive. We are built to tune into the speech. That's why singers are often the most famous member of the band.

Even if you think about musical instruments, the ones that we are most keen on are guitar, violin[23] and piano, the instruments that mimic human voice, that sound like a human voice. Same with speech.

People tend to gather around individuals with powerful, 'charismatic' voice. Someone who can deliver a message with force and emotion. That's why actors who understand how to use both body and voice shine on the big screens.

With podcasting, there is only a voice, and as much as you can learn to narrate and pronounce words, not everyone is suited to run a podcast. I know that it is a somewhat controversial statement, but we are sensitive to certain frequencies, and some people fit right into them. I would say the Host of *Casefile* is one who has a voice with the desirable frequency. He is still baffled why anyone would listen to his voice! Once he is done recording, he almost never listens back to the episode.

Study radio hosts, people who have successful auditions, the top 100 podcasts out there. Individuals who run them have one thing in common: they sound good.

I don't want to discourage anyone, but know your strengths and weaknesses. Some people are excellent writers, others look good on camera, some sound good on the radio. By all means, don't judge yourself. For that, you must break the barrier of fear and ask others for feedback. No, asking your friends or family doesn't count.

These are my arguments why podcasting is on the rise and why it will only gain in popularity. You are not late to the party, but don't wait any longer. Even though there are millions of listeners of podcasts, most of them are still based in the USA and Canada, with the British and Australian markets growing. That's a tiny fraction of the whole world.

It's a similar story with audiobooks.[24] As mobile phones have become an extension of our everyday life, these mediums are the best and easiest way to consume content.

Podcasting is still a niche market, a 'wild west' as some would say. Not much is regulated, there aren't many rules, and most of us learn as we go along. I wasn't aware of the industry before starting with *Casefile*, and I'm a sound editor! I worked on dialogue editing for movies for three years prior and it never occurred to me that podcasting was so huge.

Again, don't wait up, the time to start your show is now. With time, the space will become cluttered and it will be harder to break out. It's the same as with other mediums. How easy was it to have a favourite channel on YouTube ten years ago? Even five? I bet much easier than it is now. Let's have a look at why you should start a podcast today.

PODCASTING AS A HOBBY

You should start podcasting just because you want to see if you enjoy it. No agenda, no long-term goals, no business plans. You only want to tell stories and are looking for a new hobby, something to do at the end of the day.

I think this—of all the other reasons—is the best one because it's honest. That's how *Casefile* started, as a hobby project.

We all have hobbies, work that we do for the sake of it, and we don't call it work either. Actions that make us lose the sense of time and place that put us in a state of 'flow' as explained by psychologist Mihaly Csikszentmihalyi.[25] When I speak with my youngest brothers, I always tell them not to worry about their schooling so much, but to look for that one thing they would enjoy to do. Be it dancing, maths, design, writing, reading, anything. Not for the parents, not for the teachers, not for anyone but themselves.

I remember having quite a few hobbies like that, and I am still looking for new projects all the time. Something to learn, something to read and something that will help me to achieve the 'flow' state again.

Podcasting may be one of these projects. Not just the actual recording, but the whole process: researching, writing, recording, editing, publishing.

It takes dedication and effort to release a single episode; it's not a job for procrastinators. Do it because you love listening to podcasts, because you love telling stories, because you are looking for the next thing to obsess about. And I guarantee, when you complete your first one, there won't be any turning back.

PODCASTING AS A MARKETING TOOL

Last year I noticed that most people who are trying to develop a personal brand started a podcast. As an audio version of their YouTube channel, or an extra content created just for the medium. I'm not going to name anyone here, I don't want to sound biased, but if you are following someone online, someone who is savvy with internet marketing and has developed a following, chances are they are running a podcast.

Why is that? They must have noticed the trend. Podcasting is on the rise, and it's another way to grow a business and build a brand. If you have a business, consider podcasting as one of your marketing tools. Do you have a restaurant? You can talk about running a restaurant. Are you are a designer? You can run a show where you discuss design techniques, tricks and tips. Anything like that can strengthen your position as an expert in a field. It's similar to writing a blog or publishing a book. Take this guide as an example.

Why did I choose to write it? One reason was to fulfil my dream of writing a book, at least to start on that path—check. Second, was to position me as an authority in the field of podcasting. I doubt that I will make any money off this book, that's not the end goal. If you wanted to learn to play the guitar, what kind of a teacher would you choose? A person that lives down the street and claims to have played for ten years or someone who has a tutoring YouTube channel, students that can vouch for him and a book on how to play the guitar?

Both may be excellent teachers, but it is the second one that will attract more clients and higher fees. It's all part of marketing and podcasting can be quite helpful for the business.

PODCASTING AS A BUSINESS

The last idea is to make a podcast your primary source of income. I don't need to say that this is difficult to fulfil and only a few are able to do it. It is not impossible—if someone else has done it, then you can do it too—but take *Casefile* as an example. Our download numbers are high, we are one of the most popular podcasts around, and yet still it is not a business.

The Host has a full-time job, and the members of the team still have other projects to pay the rent. We are still learning and figuring it all out; podcasting is such a unique venture, it is not just like any other business.

I'll talk about monetising your show in another chapter, but my word of advice would be not to quit your job just yet. Start your podcast, keep at it for few months and see where it takes you. Remember that people are fickle; they may love your show one day and leave you the next one, so diversifying your income is always a good idea. Warren Buffet, one of the most successful investors, says don't rely on one income stream.

If you are one of the lucky few, then I bet that podcasting can be a fulfilling business. We'll see where *Casefile* takes us; it would be amazing if we could do it full-time, at least for a while. It is not an expectation, and at the moment our focus is to have the best audio show out there. You can't lose with thinking like that.

> **NOVEMBER 2019 UPDATE**
>
> They say that hard work pays off. I can say that *Casefile* is now also a strong business that allows us to focus on the production full-time as well as assembling a strong team. It took us a few years to get to that point, but I wouldn't want it any other way. If we can do it, then anyone can.

PODCASTING STATISTICS

I talked about podcasting being on the rise, but let's have a look at some statistics to verify the claims.

First interesting one comes from *Copyblogger*,[26] where the author (Jon Nastor) presents a brief history of podcasting, how it all started. The date is 2003, when *Radio Open Source* premieres as a first podcast, but it was 2004/2005 when it all kicked off. It was when Libsyn[27]—a podcasting service provider—started their business and iTunes[28] released a native support for podcasts.

2007 was still quite small for podcasting, though Ricky Gervais's show set the record for the most downloaded podcasts, at 261,670 downloads. Only five years later, in 2013, Apple said that podcasts had reached one billion subscribers.

Business Insider[29] claims a steady growth of the US population that listens to podcasts. According to their published article, only 9% listened to podcasts in 2008 with a jump of 21% in 2016.

Technological developments and the falling price of mobile phones are the main culprits of the trend. If you want to check it yourself, see Google Trends[30] statistics, search for 'podcast' and set the period for 'past five years'. You will notice a steady growth—not a sharp rise as some claim, but the medium is growing.

The last one would be a *TechCrunch* article[31] where they discussed the future of podcasting. They argued that, even though the format is gaining in popularity and the tools for podcast production are getting better, it is still a quite unusual business to run. According to their article, most podcasters are dissatisfied with revenue generation, the discovery of their shows and social media integration. There is still a lot to improve, and that means a lot of business opportunities.

One thing is sure, though: the experimentation has just started. Rules are not set in stone, and you can be the one who helps to shape 'the industry'. The audience is growing, ideas for monetisation are born every day and help is on the way. 'Follow the money' is the saying, but in present times we should change it to 'follow the attention'.

Podcasting attracts more listeners with each year, and it's a matter of time before it becomes regulated. The time to start is now. It's always better to sit at the table and make the rules than being late to the party.

---

19 Gutenberg Printing Press (*https://www.historyguide.org/intellect/press.html*)
20 YouTube (*n 18*)
21 Orson Welles – The War of the Worlds (*n 1*)
22 Equal Loudness Contours
 (*https://www.sfu.ca/sonic-studio/handbook/Equal_Loudness_Contours.html*)
23 The Violin (*http://hyperphysics.phy-astr.gsu.edu/hbase/Music/violin.html*)
24 Audiobook consumer 2016 (*http://www.edisonresearch.com/audiobook-consumer-2016*)
25 Mihaly Csikszentmihalyi – Flow: The Psychology of Optimal Experience
 (*http://www.goodreads.com/book/show/66354.Flow*)
26 Copyblogger – From 2003 to 2016: The Astounding Growth of Podcasting
 (*http://www.copyblogger.com/growth-of-podcasting*)
27 Libsyn (*https://www.libsyn.com*)
28 iTunes (*n 5*)
29 Business Insider (*http://uk.businessinsider.com/podcasts-are-becoming-more-popular-among-listeners-and-advertisers-2016-6*)
30 Google Trends (*https://www.google.co.uk/trends/explore?q=%2Fm%2F04058p*)
31 TechCrunch – The Future Of Podcasting
 (*https://techcrunch.com/2015/07/18/the-future-of-podcasting*)

IDEA

Everything starts with an idea, but it is the execution that drives it. Ideas are everywhere, and you probably have hundreds of them every day, however, until you take action, ideas just sit and wait in your head. I'll talk about the action plan in the next chapter, but in this one, we'll start with the first step: your concept for a podcast. Let's have a look at two important aspects of every venture; passion and practicality.

In his popular book *The 7 Habits of Highly Effective People*,[32] Stephen Covey said "start with an end in mind", meaning that even the most perfect idea will need a bit of market research too. Think about it as both a hobby and a business.

Why hobby?

It would be good to start a podcast about a subject that you enjoy, a topic with a passion and expertise that you can share with others.

Why business?

If you start a podcast as a hobby and don't do the market research, then you may end up creating a show that is similar to other podcasts. It's going to be hard to break through the crowd. Or maybe you will start a show that violates some of the iTunes[33] rules, and after all the work you will get rejected. Just because you didn't read the terms and conditions.

That's where business and marketing research comes in, to validate your idea. At the end of the day you need the balance between the two, if you jump on the recent podcasting trends and start a show without knowledge or passion, people will notice. In six months you will struggle to get the episodes out, and it will become a chore.

Look at *Casefile*, after over a year of almost non-stop work, we are still not a business; we are still learning how to run things, how to make it work. Problems and issues come up every day, and the organisation aspect of running the show often overshadows the content creation process. We still do the work. I still love talking about the show, editing the narration, scoring the episodes, mixing the show, responding to comments and helping everyone on the team.

If you don't have that intrinsic motivation, then no amount of money will buy it. Eventually, you will adapt to more cash in your bank account, and it will lose its appeal. Without the love for the project, the money won't be enough to push you forward.

Let's now answer a few questions that will help you to come up with an idea and validate it at the same time:

Is there a topic that you like to talk and read about?

I think that question should be at the centre of your idea and it goes together with the principle of passion and hobby. People will notice if you enjoy the subject of your podcast. 'Enjoy' may be the wrong word because it is hard to enjoy true crime, for example, but appreciating it makes sense: especially the research and effort to bring awareness to some cases. Write a list of things that you like, something that you pursue without an agenda.

Let's run an example; I could do one about music, books, sound, freelancing, movies, finance, video games. These are just a few things that I like to research, and any of these could be a good idea for a podcast.

Another idea: podcasting could be around your business. If you are running a venture, you can talk about it with other people. It's something that you know and do every day, easy subject to turn into a podcast. First thing would be to like the topic you wish to pursue.

Do you have expertise in a subject?

It's time to start narrowing your idea. There are plenty of things that you like, but do you have an in-depth knowledge around any of these subjects? Is there something that you can teach to others? Or do you just share a mild interest?

Expertise is in demand, and the subject doesn't matter too much. As long as you sound knowledgeable about the matter, there will be people who want to learn from you.

Remember the list of my interests? Let's narrow it down.

Although I read a lot about finance and investing, I'm not an expert by any measure and I wouldn't want to give advice to anyone; there are better-equipped people to do that.

Same with video games; I played a lot of games in the past, but I haven't gamed on my PS4 for two years now. I follow the news, but I wouldn't be able to share any deeper insights on the topic.

The sound production subject could be a good option, as I have professional training and a few years of experience behind me, same with music. That could be the right choice.

Freelancing sounds like a topic I could share some insights on, same with books and movies.

As you can see, I'm distilling the list. I recognised where I would be able to offer value and other subjects that I only have a mild interest in. Do the same with your list.

First, write as many things as you can, things that you like and enjoy. Then split them between 'expertise' and 'interest' and see what you have left. Are you prepared to read/write/talk about the subject a year or two from now? A good question, but a tough one to answer.

What happens when initial excitement passes?

Will you continue to produce content? Or will you give up?

Consider the fact that even if your podcast is extremely popular, it will still take around one or two years minimum to monetise it… and even longer to build an audience.

Let's say you discovered yoga and are into it, practising all the time, loving all the benefits you get from the workouts. You want to start a podcast about it. Do you think you will want to talk about yoga two years from now? My friend, a yoga teacher, has been doing yoga every day for eight years now. She reads books about it, she teaches classes, she takes courses. She lives and breathes yoga, it's a part of her life.

If you have something like that, then awesome, you are in luck. However, don't think that because you are interested in a subject right now, then you can have a successful podcast around it. Podcasting is a lot of work, and if you don't have a passion for the topic, it will become a routine.

Back to my list, I'm left with a few choices: sound, music, books, freelancing, movies. Which ones am I prepared to talk about for two years non-stop? I watch movies but not as many as I did in the past and I wouldn't want to spend time on researching every film. Pass.

Sound and music are obvious choices for a podcast, but am I willing to talk about it every week? It's my profession, for now, but it may change in the future, and I don't think I have enough passion for it. I could just go into niches, such as podcast production or sound editing, but will there be enough material to present? Let's leave it for now.

Freelancing and books. This sound interesting, as I'm a freelancer and a business owner at the moment, it's something I do every day so it should be an easy topic. I love reading books and have since I was a child, another subject to consider.

I'm left with a couple of maybes and two, in my opinion, good ideas. Let's move on.

Will you have enough material?

Another big one to answer. Take *Casefile*, for example; we will never run out of material to cover. Crime happens every day, this is the world we live in. There are thousands of past crimes too; it's enough material to last for decades, even if we were doing two episodes a week.

But take an example of a yoga podcast. You could bring new people in to interview each week, but soon you may start running out of ideas. Maybe you could talk about running a yoga practice? A yoga studio? But yoga itself could be a tricky subject to talk about for hundreds of episodes.

Unless you are running a seasonal podcast. Ten episodes about yoga and that's it; next season is about something else, a show on lifestyle and wellbeing.

> *Quick tip*
> Select a topic and write a minimum of fifty ideas for 'upcoming episodes'. If you struggle to come up with the list, abandon the subject.

Do some research beforehand and look for unlimited material. Otherwise, there will be a point that you will start repeating the same ideas. If you are a podcast listener, you probably know one or two shows that fell into that trap. Don't go into a topic with a closed end, or if you do, be wary of the complications.

When I look back at my list, sound and music could be a potential problem, especially if I wanted to talk about the technical aspects, such as editing, mixing and production. There is plenty of info to deliver, but three years from now I could be in trouble. Above all, if I choose a niche subject, such as a podcast on production and audio engineering, I may get bored after a while.

Freelancing and books sound okay. However, a podcast about freelancing would be problematic sooner rather than later. I could bring in people for interviews, but I doubt that general tips and advice would differ much. A show about books has more going on for it, as there is unlimited material out there.

I recommend you think about the subject in the same manner; list pros and cons, research the field and follow the objections. It's better to do it early on before you invest weeks of work in it.

What is trending?

A bit of a left turn from our list, but let's take a step back and study current trends and how your idea stacks up. The first move would be to open iTunes or iTunescharts.net[34] and examine top podcasts.

As of February 2017, I can see a lot of political podcasts, true crime, history, business, comedy shows and personal development. These are the subjects people like and want to listen to. You can also look up Top Episodes and check the most popular ones. Try switching to different countries, so you are not restricting your market.

Another tool would be to go to a website like Social Blade[35] and study YouTube,[36] Twitch,[37] Instagram[38] and Twitter.[39] Look up the most popular channels and see what people are watching and why.

Now it's a good time to test your concept. The first check is Google Trends;[40] type in your idea and look at the horizontal line, if it's a steady growth then you are onto something.

When I test sound, music, books and freelancing, first three have steady interest over a period of five years. Freelancing has an upward line, so the curiosity is growing. I can see that there are a few podcasts about business and marketing so it could be a right choice.

Remember, on iTunes you can also change the categories to do the research. Spend some time validating your idea against current trends and write it down, look for patterns.

Take *Casefile*, for example. True crime is one of the most popular genres on iTunes, so that's perfect. It means that people want to listen to that type of content. It also means that competition to be at the top is fierce and everyone wants to jump on the latest trend, with plenty of people seeing it as another business opportunity. As you learnt before, be wary of doing that.

What is the niche competition?

When you decide on the niche, it's time to look up the competition. Open iTunes and, in the search box, type in the keywords that are connected to your potential show. Analyse what comes up. When I type 'true crime', I can see the other shows that are in the same genre. There's quite a lot of them; like I said before, it's a fierce competition.

If I do it with 'yoga', I can still see quite a lot of podcasts around the subject, as you would expect with something that is quite popular nowadays. And when I test ideas from my list, I can see there is some competition in each category. The question is, should I be worried? What are other people doing? You are now diving deeper into competition research.

If you are happy with your idea, or are still trying to figure out which one is the best, check what other people in a similar field are doing. Check their podcasts, what kind of shows are they are running? Do they have a website? What about the social media presence? Don't get discouraged just because initially you see another fifty podcasts about the same subject; they may have a different style than you. It's important to check other aspects of their show and see if you can offer something better or different.

Look at the true crime genre; even though it's populated, everyone has a unique spin on the subject. There are talk shows, audio dramas, comedy shows, reviews. All about true crime. 'Scratch your itch' is good advice; learn what competitors are doing, and see if there is something that hasn't been done yet, a void that you can fill.

At the end of your research, you should have a good idea of the direction in which to take your show. Why would anyone listen to your podcast? Think about the value you can bring to the table. If there are another fifty podcasts about yoga, why should anyone listen to yours? What is unique about your show?

Let's say I want to copy the *Casefile* formula and create the same show. Same kind of narration, similar music and a familiar vibe. Would I be able to 'steal' *Casefile* fans? I doubt it. *Casefile* is now quite established, with around fifty episodes in the back catalogue. The show has a group of supporters, and if the podcast keeps the quality, it would be hard for me to 'steal' the fans.

Think about what makes you peculiar and distinctive. Think about other top podcasts too, why are these popular? We often get messages that the episodes of *Casefile* are too long, that we should keep them around 20–30 minutes. But when we look at download numbers, the most popular episodes to date are the longest ones! Being a contrarian works, don't follow the crowd.

If I were to start a podcast, one thing that would make me unique would be my accent. English is not my first language, and you can hear it straight away. Some could be drawn to it; others would skip the show because of it. It's something that is different than most shows in the charts.

I guess this is the hardest question of all, why would anyone listen to you? Given that most have the option to tune into whatever they like, why should people spend their precious time with you? What value can you offer?

As you can see it's not as easy as it sounds and that's why only the best rise to the top. The ones that love what they do and do it with excellence and passion. They have what people want. Build your show on those pillars, and there is a chance that you will break through the competition.

You should remember what I said before: people are fickle. They can bring someone up and down in the same minute; they can leave their favourites in a second if they sense any indication of dishonesty. Keep it light, have fun and get to work. The podcast is not going to produce itself.

THE NAME

I wanted to write a quick paragraph about naming your show. I will keep it short, as I know that this is the most subjective decision that you will encounter.

Make your name easy to spell and memorable. There is a rule, I'm not sure if it's true, that words with plosive letters such as 'k' are easier to remember. They have a strong and commanding sound.

Test it on your logo and banners, check if it is still readable when you minimise the logo to 30 × 30 pixels size. Decide if you want to include your name or the name of your business.

Let's say that I wanted to start a podcast around freelancing; I could call it 'Freelancing Podcast' or could use my name 'Mike's Freelancing Podcast'. I could also go with 'The Mike Migas Show', which would mean that I'm trying to create a personal brand.

I could do a few episodes on freelancing, but if I were to 'branch out' into book reviews, it would be easy to claim that it's 'The Mike Migas Show', so I can do whatever I want.

Spend some time thinking about the name but, on the other hand, don't worry about it too much. It's the content that will make your name in the long run.

Casefile didn't mean anything until it became popular.

ITUNES REQUIREMENTS

Before I finish this chapter, I wanted to give you a copy of iTunes requirements and restrictions from their site. The last thing you want is to spend hours writing and recording your episode and then be rejected by iTunes because you didn't read the rules.

Before we jump into that, I just felt I should offer up one principle that you should have in your mind while creating your show. Content can either hurt or help your brand. Every status update, every post, every episode can do wonders for you or burn you. In the age of the internet, information spreads like wildfire, and you have to be on your toes. Every time you want to post something, ask yourself a question: will it help or hurt my brand?

Enough with the questions and let's have a look at the requirements taken from the iTunes page:[41]

"Podcast artwork and all podcast content must be original and cannot contain any of the following:

- Content depicting graphic sex, violence, gore, illegal drugs, or hate themes.
- Content that could be construed as racist, misogynist, or homophobic.
- Explicit language without setting the <explicit> tag to true.
- Self-censored language in titles, subtitles, or descriptions. Instead, these metadata fields must be written as intended. All words should be completely spelled out and should not be censored. Apple Podcasts automatically censors certain explicit words in titles (for example, f**k and s**t). Don't insert the asterisks yourself unless they were included in the original title.
- Irrelevant, non-descriptive or spam content.
- Password protection.
- References to illegal drugs, profanity, or violence.
- Third-party content or trademarks without legal authorization or usage rights.
- The terms Apple Inc., Apple Podcasts, Apple Music, iTunes Store, or iTunes."

---

32 Stephen Covey – The 7 Habits of Highly Effective People
   (*https://www.stephencovey.com/7habits/7habits.php*)
33 iTunes (*n 5*)
34 iTunes charts (*n4*)
35 Social Blade (*https://socialblade.com*)
36 YouTube (*n 18*)
37 Twitch (*https://www.twitch.tv*)
38 Instagram (*https://www.instagram.com*)
39 Twitter (*https://twitter.com*)
40 Google Trends (*n 30*)
41 iTunes Resources and Help (*https://itunespartner.apple.com/en/podcasts/overview*)

GETTING STARTED

Whoever said that the first step is the hardest has never run a marathon. Unlike what some may think, podcasting is a bit like a marathon, not a sprint. Metaphors aside, starting out is difficult. It's easy to come up with a new idea; I have one every few minutes. Doing something about it requires particular character and strength to push through good and bad days. Everyone procrastinates, well, at least from the people I know. Even now, as I'm typing this paragraph, I'm pondering if I should take a break and make a cup of tea, check my emails or look at the phone one more time. It's normal, and these thoughts are here to stay; now it's easier than ever to give in to distractions.

Over the years, I have learnt a few techniques that will help you to start your project. They are nothing new, some could say they're common sense, but they work for me, so maybe they will help you to stay on track too.

ACCOUNTABILITY

The thing that works best for me is accountability. People behind *StickK* website[42] think so too. You set your goal, set the stakes, get a referee and do the work. If you fail to achieve the target, you lose the money. Now, that's what I call motivation.

I don't use the website myself, but I still use 'accountability' as my first productivity technique. Take this book, for example: I wanted to publish something for a long time and decided to start with a podcasting guide as my first step to authorship. I knew that my wants were just empty words and I needed to build accountability around the task.

First, I told my girlfriend (now wife), then I spoke with the Host, next I shared my goal with my family and friends. Finally, not only did I published a post on my social accounts, but I also included a small notice in a *Casefile* newsletter.

Most of the actions happened when I only had a summary of the book. It was still in early stages then, so if I abandoned the idea it wouldn't be a big deal. However, after sending out notifications, too many people knew about my plan, and if I stopped the project, I would have to deal with several uncomfortable questions.

"How is your book coming along?"

"When can I read it?"

"Is it out yet?"

The principle of accountability is powerful, but it may not always work. I read that sometimes, by telling people your plans, you count that as the action, success in itself, and therefore you stop. Similar to buying a gym membership, the act of signing up is enough for some people, and they never follow through.

It's all about self-awareness. Will telling others about starting a podcast help you? Or make you procrastinate even more? Test it out; there is no other way to learn.

SCHEDULE AND DEADLINES

After letting people 'in' on your project, the next tool to get you started is scheduling and setting deadlines that will keep you in check. Deadline-setting is the most useful tool when it is done right. Unfortunately, a lot of people don't approach it correctly and complain when nothing happens. It's all about setting small milestones and short-term goals.

Let's say you set a goal for releasing the first podcast three months from now. At first glance, it is a praisable aim. You have three months to complete the task, more than enough. But sooner rather than later you will find yourself procrastinating and not following through, then, in the last few weeks, you will start to panic and rush to produce your show. The minute you realise how much work is involved, you give up and return to the status quo. That is not having a podcast.

What is the other solution? Fill your schedule with mini-goals, for example:
- *first week* – the idea.
- *second week* – writing the first episode.

- *third week* – test and feedback from family.
- *fourth week* – setting up recording equipment.
- *fifth week* – learning all about hosting; and so on.

Smaller goals are easier to fulfil and will keep you motivated. At the end of each week, you will get the feeling of accomplishment, and it will keep you moving forward.

Another great way to keep motivated is to put the schedule up on the wall, so you see it all the time. On the wall behind my computer screen is a big calendar/planner where I write tasks and goals. I only need to look up to see what I have planned for the week. Behind me, I have a giant white board where I write 'big picture' plans and ideas. It's something that reminds me where I am going and why I am doing the work. Below, I have a smaller white board where I write goals for the month that I cross out once they are completed. I only need to turn my head to see it. Finally, next to me on the desk are a piece of paper and a pen. I write small tasks I want to do on that particular day. Today, which is Monday, it says: *book, score, mm, casefile post+poll, client nat, book list*. Once I'm done with the task, I cross it out.

As you can see, scheduling and planning both play a big part in my life. I know that I'm in charge of it, and can change it anytime I want, but deadlines keep me in check. I'm not suggesting to follow my style to the letter, but having a schedule when starting out with a show will keep you going during the days that you don't want to do anything.

FOCUS

The third thing to keep in mind is your focus, and it's something that I struggle with the most. Multi-tasking is a myth, and I recommend reading *Flow*[43] by Mihaly Csikszentmihalyi and *The One Thing*[44] by Gary W. Keller and Jay Papasan to understand the power of focus.

When we are centred on one thing, we direct all our energy towards it. It becomes easier to finish the task, and it takes less time to do it. However, if we keep checking our phones, look at social media or read emails, we disrupt the workflow by adding new information to the process. It then takes a few minutes to go back to that state of focus, so it is important to block out periods of a day to do the work.

When I'm working on the next *Casefile* episode, I switch off websites, email and my phone and do the work for an hour, then I have a few minutes break to check up on things and get back to work. I try to do the same with writing. I wake up earlier, check up on my latest emails, and then I get to work. I have music running in the background, and that's about it.

In an ideal world that's what every day would look like, but it doesn't, and I struggle with it all the time. When I score and bounce files, I check my social media[45] accounts. When I write, every now and again, I will jump to emails and my phone. I say to myself that I need to organise my thoughts for the next paragraph, even though I know that I work best when all the distractions are off.

The good thing is that we can recognise the faults and work to improve them. I would recommend setting an uninterrupted time in a day when you will work on your podcast. Do the research before or after, same with marketing or idea validation.

When it comes to the actual work: writing, recording and production, you need focus to get it done. Don't take my word for it, try it out yourself and see how your productivity levels jumps up.

One more thing that you should be wary of are other people. In today's world, communication is instantaneous, and it's the biggest time-consuming distraction you can imagine. Messages, calls, tags, comments, emails: they all call for your attention when you should be doing the work. When you answer the message straight away, it means that the other person is in charge of your time. It's the same with answering the calls or chatting online. Do the work first and then get back to people. How can others value your time, if you don't value it yourself?

Let's now have a look at a few things to get you started on your journey. Podcasting is all about constructing stories with the spoken word. The production of your show will be a time-consuming task and, more often than not, you will want to skip it. Writing your episodes and recording them is fun, but the quality of the final product matters too.

If you ever listened to any podcasts, you may have noticed that, for most of them, production quality is often mediocre. Why? People focus on visuals; we tend to remember images and register most with our eyes. That's why we call sound the invisible art. You only notice it when there is something wrong with it, and most people think in such a way when they produce content. Creators don't think about the correct microphone setup, the environment they record it in, external noise or editing techniques. More often, after they realised their mistakes, they will look for help to save their recording. Sometimes it's too late.

When I work with clients, I always advise on the recording setup. The reason? When you get it right at the source, you won't even need my help later on! Even with minimal equipment and knowledge, you can get decent results, and there is nothing better than a comment from a fan of 'Your podcast sounds fantastic'.

The sound is a part of life. It is around you when you wake up; it is there when you go to sleep. Most animals communicate with sound;[46] humans use it to express emotions, artistic creativity and ideas. A powerful speech, a roar of a sports car engine or chanting crowd during a big sports event: sounds ranging from quiet to deafening have a significant impact on us.

FUNDAMENTALS OF SOUND

We describe sound as changes in the atmospheric pressure.[47] Compressed air molecules cause the change to flow in the form of a wave through the atmosphere. Particles do not move with the wave, they only compress and decompress as the wave moves through a medium (air, water and others) over time.

There is a difference when sound moves through water and air, because water is denser, sound travels much faster.[48] A waveform is a graphic representation of that journey. Sound doesn't look like this in real life, a longitudinal wave is the actual description of it, but we use waveform for simplicity. Waveform's key features are amplitude, frequency, velocity, wavelength, harmonic content and envelope.

Amplitude is the easiest. It is the loudness of the wave, the value from negative to positive peak.

Frequency is the rate of the vibrations in given time. Higher frequency equals higher pitch.

Velocity is the speed of sound. It is approximately 344 m/s (1120 ft/s) through the air at 20° C (68° F). The speed is temperature dependent, and when it gets hot, the sound travels faster.

Wavelength is a physical distance between the start and the end of one wavelength cycle.

Harmonic content is the spectrum of frequencies called overtones. Not one but many frequencies create a sound, unless it is a single frequency sound.[49]

The *envelope*[50] is an individual variation that happens over time to a played sound. Envelope describes how fast sound makes a noise, how long it lasts and how quickly it quietens down.

Loudness

Loudness[51] is a general characteristic that describes the sound as either loud or quiet. But what is the measurement of loudness? And what is the human threshold of withstanding loud sounds?

Do you remember the last time when you went out to a live gig and the next day your ears were ringing? It means it was too loud.

We measure loudness by the decibel, or dB[52]. There are a lot of variations, but the most common is sound pressure level (SPL), measured in decibels. A quiet conversation will be around 40 dB, but a close-up jet engine is around 160dB. Decibel is a logarithmic value that articulates differences in force between two levels.[53] SPL is only one unit of measure, and there are others, such as voltage V and wattage W; it can get a bit complicated.

You can use SPL to describe loudness. It explains the build-up of acoustic pressure in a defined space, like a bedroom. To keep the loudness even across different formats, we have benchmarks for sound. In mixing studios, the reference is often set between 79 dB to 85 dB. The loudness will vary by a few decibels, up or down, but keep in mind the threshold for pain will start around 130 to 140 dB.[54] Gunshots are around that barrier, and that's why you can see people wearing noise-cancelling headphones at a gun range.

It is important that I mention the human ear's sensitivity to different frequencies at various levels; we describe this effect as the Fletcher-Munson curve. It is one of the studies that tries to explain our perception of sound.[55] Human sensitivity to certain frequencies will make some sounds more dominant than others, even if they are at the same loudness level. For example, a 40 Hz tone has to be about 6dB louder than a 1 kHz tone at 110 dB SPL to perceive it with the same loudness.

We are more sensitive to sounds that are within the spectrum of a human voice. The loudness can also deceive our perception of pitch and sounds with certain frequencies[56] mask other sounds. For that reason, EQ and frequency filtering are such powerful tools when it comes to mixing.

Human body
Somehow you need to hear a sound, and your body is a perfect mechanism for that. Sound pressure waves arrive at our ears, where they journey as electric impulses to our brain.

The human ear has three essential parts: the outer ear, the middle ear and the inner ear.

The *outer ear*[57] gathers and transports sound to the middle ear. It includes the pinna (ear flap) and the approximately 2 cm long ear canal. It protects the middle ear from damage and delivers sounds to the eardrum on the border with the middle ear.

The *middle ear*[58] transforms sound pressure energy into internal vibrations and compression waves. It contains an eardrum and three bones: the hammer, anvil and stirrup. The eardrum's membrane sets off the bones, and it transmits the vibrations to the fluid in the inner ear as a compression wave.

The *inner ear*[59] transforms the energy of the compression wave into nerve impulses. The cochlea and semi-circular canals play a part in that process. The real heroes are hair-like nerve cells that live on the inner surface of the cochlea. They release an electrical impulse that passes to the brain, and the brain decodes it.

The human body is sensitive, even to the most delicate sounds.[60] It also has a set of thresholds that you should take into consideration. The frequency range of hearing is between 20 Hz to 20,000 Hz. Any frequency below 20 Hz we call an infrasound and anything above 20,000 Hz is ultrasound. The kind of frequencies that we use in underwater sonars. Cats can detect frequencies as low as 45 Hz and as high as 85,000 Hz.

The barriers to watch out for are the threshold of hearing, feeling and pain. The loudest sound possible is around 194 dB, but you will lose your hearing at 180 dB! Wear earplugs when working with loud sounds; some earplugs can make the music more enjoyable and clearer.

Now that you understand a bit about fundamentals of sound, let's talk some action. First of all, thank you for reading through the last couple of pages. I always say that even a basic knowledge of the subject will help in the long run. Podcasting is all about the sound, so it's a good investment to learn a bit about the physics of the medium. Once you have the knowledge, it's time to take the first step.

Write a test script
At this stage, I wouldn't write a full episode yet. Writing an entire episode requires time and research, and for now, you need to test the idea.

Let's say you want to start a book review podcast. To do the test episode, if I were you, I would pick up a book that I know well, write a few bullet points on paper and a general structure I want to follow. Last year, my partner and I decided to start a YouTube[61] show (it's gone now, don't try to find it) and to test it I wrote a short test script, a few bullet points. It took me few minutes, and we were ready to go.

Record a test script
Next step is to record yourself. This move is made before you invest in recording equipment and any other gear. What I'd like you to do is use your mobile phone or a voice recorder on your laptop and record a short 'podcast' based on your test script. Come up with an intro, main content and outro. I could say keep it under a few minutes; however, most podcasts are around thirty minutes on average. It's easy to sound exciting for three minutes but can you do it for thirty? Don't worry about the quality or mistakes for now. Remember, you are just testing if you even enjoy podcasting.

Going back to my story about starting a YouTube channel, we recorded a 'test' episode with a mobile phone; it was quite awkward and harder to do than we thought. You will experience the same thing (unless you are a born podcaster, then congratulations!), but don't worry: you are starting out, and everyone needs to start somewhere.

When you finish the recording, I would also recommend doing a quick sound edit. Find some theme music to play at the beginning, maybe an outro too. Treat it as if you would be releasing the episode for real. It will give you a glimpse of editing and post-production work; you can't run from it.

Spend an evening working on your 'pilot', polish it and make it sound good but also don't delay, and don't get distracted by perfectionism. Give yourself a deadline of one evening to write, record and produce. Block out the distractions and get to work.

> *Quick tip*
> Not every podcast has to be scripted. Comedy shows, talk shows, business interviews are only a few examples where 'script' is not needed. It all depends on the direction you want to take with the show.

Feedback

Now for the last part. Listen to your show; you may love it, you may hate it, but it doesn't matter. It's time to ask for feedback. It's the hard part; you created something, and people can criticise it. They won't care how much work you put into the episode; they don't know how passionate you are. Get used to it.

I would suggest asking your friends and family for feedback. Get a few people to listen to it, send it over to them. Tell them to treat it as if it wasn't you, that you are looking for an honest opinion. Truth be told, the feedback will be biased. There is no way that your close ones will provide neutral feedback; they know you, and they know your voice. If you are brave, post your recording on the internet. There are plenty of groups and forums where you can ask people for feedback.

Would I do it? Probably not with the 'test' episode. You may be different; you may be stronger than me. Strangers on the internet are merciless and sometimes can get to you.

Remember that you are just testing it. The script was written in ten minutes, you recorded it on your phone, and you produced it in a couple of hours. Don't expect love and praise from outsiders, and that's why I think asking friends and family for the first feedback is better to break that wall. Podcasting is about doing what you want to do, no matter what other people say.

I rarely read *Casefile* reviews and try not to Google the show. Yes, we get criticism all the time. Am I used to it? I don't think I'll ever be. People want to be liked, and I'm no different. Constructive feedback is important, getting used to feedback is crucial. Stopping your work because of criticism? Never.

Guess what? You've just recorded your first podcast, yes it was a 'pilot', but you have done it. It will be smooth sailing from now on. Just kidding, start preparing for war.

---

42 StickK (*https://www.stickk.com*)
43 Mihály Csíkszentmihályi – Flow (*n 25*)
44 Gary Keller – The One Thing (*http://www.the1thing.com*)
45 Facebook (*n 2*)
46 How well do dogs and other animals hear? (*http://www.lsu.edu/deafness/HearingRange.html*)
47 Sound is a pressure wave
   (*http://www.physicsclassroom.com/class/sound/Lesson-1/Sound-is-a-Pressure-Wave*)
48 How does sound in air differ from sound in water?
   (*http://www.dosits.org/science/soundsinthesea/airwater*)
49 Overtones and harmonics (*http://hyperphysics.phy-astr.gsu.edu/hbase/music/otone.html*)
50 Envelope (*http://www.britannica.com/science/envelope-sound*)
51 The relationship of voltage, loudness, power and decibels
   (*http://www.gcaudio.com/resources/howtos/loudness.html*)
52 Decibels (*http://artsites.ucsc.edu/ems/music/tech_background/te-06/teces_06.html*)
53 Equal Loudness Contours
   (*http://www.sfu.ca/sonic-studio/handbook/Equal_Loudness_Contours.html*)
54 Noise reduction ratings explained (*http://www.coopersafety.com/noisereduction.aspx*)
55 How Do We Perceive Sound? (*https://www.youtube.com/watch?v=Z2-WD16DXtQ*)
56 What is up with Noises? (*https://www.youtube.com/watch?v=i_oDXxNeaQo*)
57 Outer Ear (*http://www.asha.org/public/hearing/Outer-Ear*)
58 Middle Ear (*http://www.asha.org/public/hearing/Middle-Ear*)
59 Inner Ear (*http://www.asha.org/public/hearing/Inner-Ear*)
60 Hearing & Balance: Crash Course A&P #17 (*https://www.youtube.com/watch?v=Ie2j7GpC4JU*)
61 YouTube (*n 18*)

FIRST EPISODE

The first one is important: it's the one that people, in the beginning, will go to, the one that 'defines' your podcast.

On the other hand, the first one doesn't matter as much. We often cringe when we think about the first few episodes of *Casefile*, even though I did re-master them later on. The sound quality was less than mediocre, the narration was lacking, the mix was all over the place. We are going strong with each new case, improving on research and production and gaining new fans every day. The past does not define the future. Episode one was good enough to get people interested, but it didn't determine the direction of the whole show. It's all about the balance.

Spend time to make your first one as good as possible, however, stick to deadlines and forget about perfectionism. It's better to release something than nothing at all.

We all fall into the trap of little changes and improvements. You record something, then listen to it the next day and want to change it and then again and again and again. Till you get fed up with it.

I was like that too, everything had to be perfect or it would drive me crazy. I would focus on imperfections rather than see the big picture. I have learnt that it is the big vision that matters; believe me, listeners are quite forgiving. When you have a decent sound and a good story, most will enjoy your show.

I'm all about the production and making *Casefile* the best sounding podcast there ever was, but on the other hand, it is almost a weekly show. I can't spend an unlimited amount of time tinkering with the mix. Once I'm happy with the result, I move on.

At my previous job my boss—one of the best dialogue mixers in the country—told me, "If it sounds good, then it is good." I always have that in the back of my mind when I'm mixing.

Don't obsess over the first episode that much, and start with the idea. Choose something that you know well, something that comes easily to you and then dive into it. Research the competition and know your audience. For example, with *Casefile* we try not to cover cases that were done by other podcasts, as we want to offer something different. Let's say you want to start a book review podcast and have a perfect book for the first episode.

Did someone do a show on it before?

Was it popular?

What was the style of the podcast?

Can you add value to the topic?

Look, most of the ideas are not original. It's all about remixing and putting your spin on the story: that's how you make it interesting. Think about the true crime genre; for centuries, if not longer, people were interested in horrifying and disturbing stories. It's not something that we came up with on *Casefile*.

Rather than trying to think of something that hasn't been done before, take a subject and make it your own. Of course, if you go into a crowded space then you better find something that stands out.

Do we need another political podcast?

Will you offer new insights on the topic?

Let your first episode address these issues, but also plan long term. You will develop a style with time.

NAMES AND NUMBERS

An excellent idea is to plan for the names and numbering of the episodes in advance. You can change it later on your hosting services, but it's better to do it well from the start. I think numbers help to keep the order and your listeners will find it easier to differentiate the latest and the oldest episodes.

With *Casefile* we go by cases. Each case has a number, and when we run a mini-series, we add another number at the end of the name to indicate that.

A standalone episode would look like this:

Case 44: Peter Falconio

A case that is split into parts:
Case 37: Yorkshire Ripper (Part I)
And for any other updates or messages, no numbers:
End of Year Message

Most podcasting apps won't display the full name of your episode, so make sure that a good description covers that. You can start with a hashtag, with a number, whatever you like. Make it consistent and test it on the artwork. Try to keep the words to a minimum. Some people go for longer naming, that's fine. Remember, though, that most people will view your podcast on a mobile phone and your priority should be to make it look good on a small screen.

Another quick tip would be to indicate what the episode is about in the title.

If I name an episode 'Episode 1: Online Marketing', it doesn't say much to you. What aspect of online marketing? All platforms or just a specific one? It just raises too many questions, but if I name it 'Episode 1: Facebook Sponsored Posts', straight away you have the idea what the podcast is about. I could narrow it down even more, to a particular industry or business. Pay attention to naming; don't leave it until the end.

NAMING AND KEYWORDS

One more thing about the naming, be aware of suitable keywords. If you were to start a podcast around a popular topic, you might want to include keywords in the name of the episode. That applies less to the name of your show, but it can help.

I realised only recently that when I type 'true crime' or 'crime' into iTunes's[62] search box, *Casefile* comes up as the first one. I never knew that! And why is that? The full name of the show is *Casefile True Crime*, so it is the obvious result for the keyword. Happy coincidence, but it sure helps!

Include searchable keywords but don't make it sound weird. The content will make the name in the long run, not the other way around. With episodes, you will have more freedom, because you hopefully get to do a lot of them. If you create a podcast in the marketing space, it would be a good idea for your episode to show up when someone looks for a topic that you just covered.

How to find the right keywords? You will need a Google account to do that. Once you have it, Google 'keyword planner' and click on 'Keyword Research & Strategy with Keyword Planner[63] – Google AdWords' and sign in to your account. On the menu click on the Tools tab and go to Keyword Planner. There, you can look up topics and see how many people are searching for it.

In the 'Find new keywords' search box, type in the name you were considering for your episode. The results will show you the average monthly search for that keyword in Google as well as similar ideas.

I know that the info is from Google, but people who are looking in the search engine will look for similar content on iTunes. It's all about the answers and solutions; the medium doesn't matter. I would suggest, with time, diving deeper into 'keyword research' material. Some blogs and courses teach you all the techniques that will become useful once you will start a website or run a blog.

WRITING THE FIRST EPISODE

How you write your first episode depends on the style of your show and the way you work. The general idea is to spend a bit of time—more than usual—doing the research and making sure the writing flows.

With podcasts like *Casefile*, it means reading and watching multiple sources of information and putting it all together into a coherent script. I don't need to say that it's a difficult task and, with long and complicated episodes, we must do it in a way that the listener isn't lost halfway through.

It will be similar to an audio drama; you will need to write a satisfying and enjoyable story, and the scripted episode will be the best way to do it. With interview-style podcasts there's much less scripting but more time is spent on research and providing your guest with interesting questions. That kind of podcast will need more work in post-production than recording because the way a guest speaks or answers is beyond your control. Don't worry, you can try to fix it during the editing process.

When you have two or more hosts running the show and talking about a subject, it's also a good tactic to know/write the topics that each one of you will cover. With time, you will learn how to improvise and answer on the spot, but if you have no previous experience of doing such things you will end up either repeating the same idea or jumping from subject to subject.

Preparation is the key. If you think that you can grab a microphone, talk for thirty minutes and become famous, I have bad news. Unless you are a born talent—and I don't believe in talent as much—you will go against thousands of people who do just that. There must be more than 500,000 podcasts out there. Again, ask the important question: why should anyone listen to you?

Preparation will give you a peace of mind and comfort in knowing that you are ready. It's false thinking to believe you can 'fix it later in the mix', and you are going to hate yourself later for that. If you are new to this, it will be a chore and more than likely you will be looking for an audio editor to help you. Which means spending money where you shouldn't have to, not in the beginning. There will be other things for you to worry about, such as setting up recording equipment, hosting, website, social media, artwork, marketing and so on. If you have never done it before, it will take you some time to learn it all, and by having your episode as good as it gets, at least you know that you have covered the main aspect. It's all about the content.

As much as I'm into perfecting the production, the recording techniques and the business side of things, *Casefile* wouldn't be so big without the Host's research, writing and narration. Even the first episodes, which didn't have perfect production values, still receive fantastic feedback. It's a lesson that you should take to heart. Fans and listeners are forgiving; if you offer them an interesting and exciting story, they (albeit with some complaints) won't hate you for lack of production value.

By all means, excellent production helps you to stand out and to keep the listeners in the long run, but it's the story that counts. If your content is lacking, no matter how much money you throw at it and how much time you spend on the production, you won't get far. If your content is gold, then production will help it to shine brighter. Keep that in mind while working on your first episode.

How scripted it will be is up to you. If I were to start my podcast tomorrow, I would approach writing just like I do with all my material, be it an essay, blog, or this book. I would lay down the structure, main points and topics and even sentences under each point. If I were to have a more laid-back show, I would probably leave it at that, although in the beginning, I would script as much as I could.

Last year, I recorded a video course and a few other videos for YouTube.[64] The course was scripted, and I memorised all the lines before recording. For a YouTube channel, it was the same for a few weeks, but after I got comfortable with the camera, I wrote less and carried the story on the spot. I would write a general structure with a few bullet points and fill the gaps in during the recording.

Learn the easiest and most comfortable way for you, but I will repeat it again: it's all about the content, it can either hurt or help your brand.

Before I finish this chapter, let's quickly talk about the actual recording. Practice your script, read it out loud a few times, record a 'test' run. Listen to the recording; can you improve the sound at the source?

It takes time to get the 'perfect' take, don't shy away from recording a line or two a few times. Worst-case scenario is that you can edit the recording in the mix. Give yourself time and don't rush it. Remember, once your episode is out there, it's open to criticism, and if deep down you know that you skipped over something, other people will notice it too.

When I work on *Casefile* I don't think about the past episodes and I don't focus on the future ones. I'm focused on making the current one the best I can so it can stand on its own.

No matter how much work you put in, you will get criticism. But if you practice your craft every day, experiment and improve, then negative feedback won't hurt as much. You will know that, at that moment in time, you did the best you could.

---

62 iTunes (*n 5*)
63 Google Keyword Planner (*https://adwords.google.com/KeywordPlanner*)
64 YouTube (*n 18*)

RECORDING EQUIPMENT

START MINIMALISTIC

In this chapter, I'm going to geek out a bit. I want to show you what you need to start a podcast, and that you don't need a lot. For the most basic setup you will require:

- *a microphone* – to capture your voice.
- *a lead* – a cable to connect the microphone.
- *a recorder* – a device that will record your voice.
- *headphones/speakers* – to listen back to your recording.

You will want to transfer the recorded audio into a computer, either from an SD card or external drive. By all means, you can record straight to your system, which is the most common scenario.

Another important issue is software, a computer program that you will use to record and edit a podcast. There are many options out there, but a word of advice would be to choose something with a user-friendly interface and all the necessary tools to do the job from start to finish. I will present free and paid options and what I use for *Casefile*.

I understand that when you start something new you want the best gear and want it now. Most people are like that, including me. Plugins, microphones, software, keyboards – I wanted it all! With time, I have learnt that I only need few tools to do good work. I've selected the bare minimum for my needs and decided to learn it inside out. I would suggest you do the same.

Great content is your mission, so become a specialist, not a generalist. Remember that you want to create a podcast, not start an audio equipment store. I'll come back to it later, but I also want to give you a few guidelines so you can avoid choice paralysis. When people have too many options, they get stuck and abandon the venture. Equipment is important, but not that important, so let's get it over with!

Here, I will talk about the technical aspects of each element of your setup. I don't want to bore you, but I think it is important to understand the basics, so please stay with me.

MICROPHONE

You need a microphone to record your podcast. Period. A microphone transforms acoustic energy—your voice—into electrical energy, which is then converted into digital files on your computer.

Three main elements make up a microphone:

I. *Transducer*

First one is a transducer, which transforms the energy. How a microphone registers your voice depends on its transducer, and there are two main types of transducers – condenser and dynamic.

Dynamic

A dynamic mic operates on a small electrical generator built from a diaphragm, voice coil and magnet. When you record a podcast, the force of your voice, as a sound wave, makes a diaphragm vibrate. I would describe the diaphragm as a thin membrane hidden behind the microphone's metallic mesh.

At the rear of the diaphragm is a voice coil—a coil of wire—that vibrates. A small magnet forms a magnetic field around that wire. The movement of the coil within the magnetic field generates electrical signals that correlate with the force of your voice.

Dynamic microphones can survive in the toughest environments, and they are the number one choice for live performance. They are not as sensitive as condensers but require more gain on the input, which often results in a higher noise floor.

Condenser

Condenser microphones are a bit more complicated than dynamic and more sensitive.

The basics of a condenser mic lie in a capacitor. The force of your voice will resonate a thin metal or metal-coated membrane that sits in front of a rigid backplate. The space between the two contracts and the motion produces electrical signals.

The biggest difference between a dynamic and a condenser is that the latter requires additional power to run. There are two ways to power up a condenser microphone. First one is with batteries, second is with phantom power. Phantom power runs through the microphone cable from the interface (e.g. the mixing desk or audio interface).

Condenser microphones are sensitive and delicate; they will pick up more noise than their dynamic siblings.

One feature of condensers that you should be aware of is the maximum sound level. Maximum sound level specification means that if you shout into a condenser and reach the threshold, there is a high probability that the recording will distort, so watch out for the levels.

Condensers are great in capturing a wide dynamic and frequency range. Try recording an acoustic guitar with a condenser and then with a dynamic microphone. You will hear that condenser captures the smallest nuances and movements of the guitar.

With condensers, you must remember that they will need extra power and require less gain on the input than dynamic microphones. They are more sensitive than dynamics, and if you record in a bedroom, you may have some acoustic issues to tackle.

II. Frequency response

The second feature is frequency response. Frequency response and range 'decide' how the recorded sound will sound. We choose microphones for their characteristics; some add more 'bottom' to the recording, others 'warmth' or 'presence'. Yes, these are technical terms.

III. Directionality

Directionality is the last element of a microphone. Directionality describes the most sensitive part of a microphone; polar patterns explain it in detail. You will find quite a few polar patterns, with the most popular being:

Omnidirectional

The omnidirectional microphone will register sound at all angles. The polar pattern covers 360 degrees. It means it will pick up the sound from the back as well as from the front and sides, with the same power.

These are great if you want to capture an ambience of a place, something like an inside of a cave. These are not the best for recording a podcast or audiobook, though.

Unidirectional

As you probably guessed, unidirectional microphones will register sounds from one particular direction, more than from others. Most popular will be a cardioid, a heart-shaped polar pattern, and it works great when you need the focus.

For example, if you wish to record dialogue on set you don't want to capture a technical crew that is chatting in the corner. Unidirectional microphones are made for this kind of stuff. It will also be the one to use for your podcast.

Bidirectional

Bidirectional microphones are sensitive at front and back but omit material from the sides. They are ideal for vocal duets and individual stereo recording techniques such as mid-side, M-S. We use this polar pattern when we want to dismiss unwanted sources of sound. It's also excellent for recording two people facing each other.

My advice? Go with cardioid and be careful with omnidirectional microphones, these may be too sensitive. So the question is, what should you choose? There are so many options!

If you are serious about podcasting, you will need to sound good. However, you don't need to spend thousands on a microphone. I will narrow it down to three options:
- a USB microphone
- an external recorder
- a microphone that requires a preamplifier – an audio interface.

All three have their pros and cons.

> **Quick tip**
> If you are looking at it as just a hobby and a side project, then a simple USB microphone may be the best solution. Read the reviews and test a few, if possible.

USB microphone
USB microphones are all-in-one solutions. They have an audio interface inside, meaning that not only do they transform acoustic energy into electrical, but inside there is an analog-to-digital converter. It turns your voice into digital information. Depending on the USB microphone, you will have a range of options available; polar patterns, gain, frequency cuts, headphone output and so on.

External recorder
An external recorder is something like a Zoom H4N.[65] It's a good solution to record interviews and sound in different locations. Apart from built-in microphones, you can connect additional external mics. It has phantom power for condensers, lots of options and you can use it as USB audio interface. I don't want it to sound like an advert. There are many external sound recorders so research as many as you can; I used Zoom H4N for field recordings, hence why I recommend it.

The "pro" setup
The last one is a 'pro' setup. A microphone connected to an audio interface, which is then linked to a computer. That's how studios record voice actors, musicians, foley.

Which option is best for you? Well, it depends on your podcast. If you decide to go out and record interviews, then an external sound recorder will be the best option. You may still need to invest in extra microphones, such as a boom mic, or you could buy a lavalier—a clip microphone—for the other person.

If you are planning on something similar to *Casefile*, an 'audio drama' kind of a podcast, then I would recommend a stationary setup. A USB mic would be a good start.

Make sure that you research the type of the microphone you want to buy. Most of the USB microphones are condensers. They are easy to operate, but they will pick up background noise; the hiss, the rumble. What I would suggest is to opt in for a dynamic USB microphone. Dynamics are not as sensitive, they require more gain, but it will minimise background noise.

Downside? With more gain, you will get more hiss, and you will need a basic knowledge of cleaning that up. Amazon[66] has a return option; if you don't like the gear, then swap it for something else. You can get a starter microphone for up to a hundred dollars; it won't break the bank.

At the end of this chapter, I will give you a list of recommended gear and how much it could all cost.

CABLES

You will need cables, or as we audio geeks call them—leads. Unfortunately, the sound has not yet gone wireless, so I want to give you a few tips on selecting the right cables.

What you need to know is the difference between balanced and unbalanced cables; you might have heard about them before.

Unbalanced

Unbalanced cables have two wires inside, but only one to carry the signal, the other one is a screen wire, or ground, shield. It helps to protect the carrying wire from unwanted interference. It is fine up to 15–20 feet (4.5–6 meters), more than that and it will be prone to Radio Frequency Interference. A 'hum' that will amplify along with the wanted signal. A ¼ inch jack or phono RCA connectors are usually unbalanced. These are used for instruments, effects and other line level signals.

Balanced

Balanced cables are more interesting than their unbalanced siblings. They contain three wires inside, one screen/ground and two signal wires. These cables will run up to 50 meters / 164 feet and still produce great results. They will still pick up Radio Frequency Interference, but remove it through split phase circuitry. Now, it may get complicated.

You have three pins: positive (hot), negative (cold) and ground. A signal is split into two signals and the second one is flipped upside down. It has its phase reversed, and it becomes negative. Now you have one positive and one negative signal, if you combine them together they will cancel each other out, but because they travel on separate wires, they are fine.

Both signals pick up Radio Frequency Interference (noise) on the way. Upon reaching the preamp at the end of the cable, the negative signal is flipped back to positive, and both signals (now positive) reinforce each other as one signal.

BUT

The noise both wires picked up on the way is gone.

Why?

When the negative signal is flipped upside down, the noise on wire one becomes opposite phase to the noise on the other side, and they cancel each other out!

So do you always need a balanced cable? Absolutely not. Not all equipment will have the means to flip the phase and will always carry an unbalanced signal, so there is no need for balanced cables. When you use unbalanced cables for a balanced signal, you will get the same noise as you would with an unbalanced signal.

> ***Quick tip***
> If you are looking at it as just a hobby and a side project, then a simple USB microphone may be the best solution as it comes with all necessary cables. Read the reviews and test a few, if possible.

AUDIO INTERFACE

The best way to describe audio interface is that it is an external sound card for your system. You may ask, I have a sound card on my laptop, why would I need to spend extra money on an audio interface?[67] A standard sound card in a computer is quite basic; it's okay when you want to listen to music or talk on Skype, but audio interface means that you are serious about podcasting.

First of all, it will improve the sound capabilities of the system. It will give you a better representation of recorded sounds, and it will handle further audio processing. Multiple audio tracks will crash your system, but an audio interface will handle that issue.

The most basic functions of an audio interface are recording sound and direct monitoring of a sound. The recording means that you can plug in a microphone or an instrument and record via an audio interface. What about a USB microphone, if it connects straight to the computer? That's correct, but as I mentioned before, USB microphones have a built-in audio interface. You won't need an additional interface if you purchase a USB microphone.

The audio interface lets you connect a microphone via XLR cable. A standard interface has an A-D converter (analog-to-digital). It will transform acoustic energy from the microphone into digital going into the computer. Microphones have a weak signal. Therefore, they require additional amplification, and you will find input gain control on an audio interface as well as phantom power for the condenser microphones.

Apart from that, an audio interface will often have line inputs for connecting instruments, as well as MIDI, optical ADAT or S/Pdif. These shouldn't concern you in the beginning; they are for connecting external equipment.

Let's talk about direct listening. To listen with monitors, I need to connect them via balanced cables to correct outputs. Depending on the interface, you can have stereo (two) or multiple outputs, like 5.1 surround. Other outputs will be for headphones; you will need a small to big jack adapter to plug them in.

USB interfaces are the most common one on the market. You can still find FireWire interfaces, however, with new systems like iMac, you will need a FireWire to Thunderbolt adapter to run the interface. I assume that in the future there will be more direct Thunderbolt interfaces.

So, do you need an audio interface? If you are serious about recording and want to produce a quality podcast then absolutely. Audio interfaces come with software that gives you more control over sound, and it's standard equipment in professional audio production.

However!

If you are just starting out, then go with a USB microphone. It will cost less, and as I said before, you will get an all-in-one. Be wary that quality may not be as good as you thought and there will be limitations to overcome.

> **Quick tip**
> If you are looking at it as just a hobby and a side project, then a simple USB microphone may be the best solution as it has a built-in audio interface. Read the reviews and test a few if possible.

SPEAKERS AND HEADPHONES

Even though most people listen to a podcast on mobile phones (and ear-in headphones), it's a good practice to have a pair of speakers to test your audio. The only difference you should know when you are starting out is the distinction between loudspeakers and studio monitors.

Loudspeakers

The most common loudspeakers will be your computer speakers. These are not good for anything beyond watching YouTube videos. I never test *Casefile* on laptop speakers. Given their frequency range (which is tiny) the music is inaudible, and you can only hear the narration. The podcast is all about the atmosphere; instead, I focus on making it sound good on headphones, even the cheap ones.

Then you have external loudspeakers. You can get cheap USB speakers or invest in more expensive equipment for the system. Speakers like that are excellent for listening to music, watching movies, gaming, learning. They are also useful for referencing sound mixes.

Studio monitors

And the third option – studio monitors. They may not look as fancy as conventional loudspeakers, but they are designed to give the most accurate representation of sound. That's why professionals use them for recording, mixing and monitoring. They are more expensive than traditional loudspeakers, and top monitors can cost thousands of dollars, per speaker.

You get a choice between passive and active monitors. Passive means you will need an external amplifier for power, active monitors have an amplifier inside. Studio monitors output a balanced signal, a clean, noise-free audio. They often have adjustment options at the back, for frequencies.

Let's say that after measurement you have learnt that your room reflects a lot of high frequencies. You could adjust them at the back of the monitors so, in the room, the sound from the monitors will be neutral. In reality, you won't need monitors unless you are mixing music, movies or doing high-profile work. I use my monitors to listen back to *Casefile* mixes, but my priority is to make the show sound good on headphones.

Headphones

At last, headphones. For any dialogue recording, be it audiobook or podcast, headphones are a must. Most people will consume your content on headphones, and even if they don't, good headphones will give you the most detailed representation of your recording.

The cheapest way is to use ear-ins. I don't recommend them for work. Use them to reference your audio, but you won't be able to catch mistakes, distortion or noise with cheap ear-ins. They are designed for listening to music and will often alter the sound.

You want to get headphones like the Sony MDR-7506.[68] They offer clear, neutral and detailed sound, and are not that expensive. They are also closed-cup, meaning they will cover your ears completely, which will allow you to hear what is going on with the recording. Every lip smack, every click will become audible; you will become aware of the noise of the floor that torments a lot of beginners.

If you are using an audio interface, you will need an adapter for the headphones. I use Sony headphones for production and mixing of the show, and

I will also play back the episode on five different kinds of ear-in headphones, from the cheapest to more expensive. Remember that most people listen on ear-ins they got with their mobile phone. Make your podcast sound good on the standard equipment, and it will sound amazing everywhere!

> **NOVEMBER 2019 UPDATE**
>
> As the show got more popular, I was lucky enough to be able to upgrade my studio as well. I still use Sony MDR-7506 headphones; however, I only use them for editing. For the mix I now use AKG K712 Pro, which are open, over-ear headphones. They are more expensive but, in my opinion, perfect for mixing and mastering.

OTHER GEAR

Pop shield and reflection shield

Other equipment that you should invest in is a pop shield (a must!) and maybe a reflection shield. A pop shield will reduce pops and mouth noises; it breaks the force of the air and makes the recording clearer. Pop shields are cheap and will save you a lot of headaches.

Reflection shields will help to minimise reflections in a room, which I assume will not be acoustically treated. If you have extra cash, the acoustic shield could be a good investment to make your recordings sound better.

Software

Choosing the right software is an important task. After all, it's the tool that you will end up using for the majority of the time. The best way is to ask yourself, what do you want from your software? And how complicated will your podcast be?

If you are looking at it as just a hobby, a side project, then a simple program may be the best solution. If you wish to produce a show similar to *Casefile*, then you will need a lot more.

Just to give you a rough estimate, my software, with the plugins I use, is worth around $4,000, if not more. You won't need to spend anywhere near that, so let's have a look at options.

Free

You can start with free options, such as Audacity,[69] which is an open-source, free audio production software. A lot of people use Audacity for audiobook production and podcasts. However, I would not recommend it. I used it for a bit and, unfortunately, it did not speak to me. By all means try it out, but there are better options for audio production.

Another one is Apple GarageBand.[70] It's basic, but it will get the job done, and it comes with a range of effects and loops. *Casefile*'s anonymous Host is not a producer or audio guy, and he uses GarageBand for his recordings. He records the narration in the software and sends me the session. I then export the audio and edit it in my software. I don't use GarageBand myself, but I would recommend it if you are just starting out.

And the last one on the list is Pro Tools First.[71] I use a professional version of Pro Tools[72] for my work, but the good guys at Avid created a free version for beginners. I would recommend learning Pro Tools from the start, PT First has enough options to get you going, and if you choose to pursue a journey into sound production, you can always switch to the pro version. When you understand the software, the switch will be much easier.

Paid

I did use a few audio sequencers in the past but I wanted to focus on just two, Apple Logic[73] and Avid Pro Tools.

If you are the owner of an Apple computer then you have probably heard of Apple Logic, it's their flagship audio program. I used it for years before moving everything to Pro Tools. Apple Logic is intuitive and helpful when it comes to music production. In the past, I used Logic to create music and Pro Tools to edit the dialogue. Logic is a powerful solution, and I would recommend checking it out.

Avid Pro Tools is the software I use for everything, and it is an industry standard. If you ever work in a recording studio, post-production house or dubbing facility, then you will encounter Pro Tools. It's fast, reliable and gets the job done. It may take you a while to learn it inside out, but if you wish to have a top-notch podcast, then I would pick Pro Tools. They have a subscription program, and you can cancel after you stop using it.

Before I get shouted at, I know that there are many other audio sequencers and most of them are more than enough to produce a podcast. The other ones that I did use were Cakewalk's Sonar,[74] Steinberg Cubase,[75] FL Studio,[76] Ableton Live,[77] Adobe Audition.[78] Don't take my word as gospel, do a diligent research and try out as many different audio solutions as you can. Play with demos and free versions, select the one that you like the most. It takes a lot of work to produce a good sounding podcast, and the tools are there to help, not to stand in your way.

Don't spend too much money; in the beginning, try free options and see if podcasting is for you. When you catch the bug, after a few episodes, and you are be hungry for more, only then start looking at more professional solutions.

One more thing. The principles of recording, editing and post-production will always be the same. The things that you are on the lookout for are the interface, the environment and how fast you can produce a show. You can always switch the programs. Once you learn how one works, you will be able to work in most of them without issues.

WHAT TO BUY

Thanks to the internet, content distribution is almost free, and you only need to invest time in learning. It's the equipment that will cost you, but again, you can get decent results on the budget.

For podcasts, audiobooks or screen capture tutorials, you want to reduce reflections of a room and find the best microphone. Acoustic booth, audio interface and an excellent mic are preferable, but you can upgrade in the future. When you start, you will probably be looking at USB mics.

You must understand that USB condensers are extremely sensitive. I assume that you will record either in a bedroom or office with windows, neighbours and passing cars. These microphones are easy to operate but will pick up the background noise, the hiss, the rumble, so be careful. What

I would suggest is to opt in for a dynamic USB microphone. You can get a starter microphone for up to 100 dollars.

Pop shield

If you decide to go with a condenser, a pop shield is a must. Even with a dynamic microphone, it will help, and you can get one for a few dollars.

Stand and cables

Most of the USB microphones come with small desk stands and cables; you don't have to spend money on that yet.

Reflection shield

If you are using a condenser, a reflection shield will help you out. Less with dynamic, but get it if you have spare cash in your pocket. You can get one for $100. Reflection shields will minimise the reflections in your room and help to control the sound. However, if you are going for a USB mic, check how easy it will be to set up the shield around it. You may need additional stands for that.

Headphones

Having an accurate representation of sound is crucial. Sony MDR-7506 headphones are a standard at ACX Amazon audiobook company.[79] These are perfect for monitoring and editing dialogue. They will set you back around 50–60 dollars so, again, not that bad. I would also invest in few cheap ear-in mobile headphones to reference mixes, so another $20 to spend.

- USB mic – less than 100 dollars
- Pop shield – 5 dollars
- Headphones – 50 dollars
- Ear-in phone headphones (2 pairs) – 20 dollars
- Reflection shield (+ stands if needed) – 100 dollars

On top of that, start with free software such as Audacity, Garage Band or Pro Tools First, or any other free demos. If you want to deliver decent quality, it's a start.

The downside to that is that you will still get some noise and echo, among other issues. Another part of the equation is education on sound production basics: don't dismiss it as nuance!

> **NOVEMBER 2019 UPDATE**
>
> Podcasting is on the rise and because of that there are more exciting solutions for both hardware and software.
>
> Hardware-wise the biggest release is Rodecaster Pro from Rode, which is all-in-one solution for podcasters. *Casefile*'s Host has one and we are using it for recording interviews, bonus content and other material.
>
> Software-wise, we now have a plethora of solutions, such as Hindenburg or Descript, which combines audio and word editing and makes it very easy to do!
>
> Do your own research, but the options look better than ever.

---

65 Zoom equipment store (*https://www.zoom.co.jp*)
66 Amazon (*http://www.amazon.com*)
67 Focusrite equipment store (*https://www.focusrite.com*)
68 Sony (*http://www.sony.co.uk*)
69 Audacity (*http://www.audacityteam.org*)
70 Garage Band (*http://www.apple.com/uk/mac/garageband*)
71 Pro Tools First (*http://www.avid.com/pro-tools-first*)
72 Pro Tools (*http://www.avid.com/pro-tools*)
73 Apple (*http://www.apple.com*)
74 Cakewalk (*http://www.cakewalk.com*)
75 Steinberg (*https://www.steinberg.net/en/products/cubase/start.html*)
76 FL Studio (*https://www.image-line.com/flstudio*)
77 Ableton (*https://www.ableton.com/en*)
78 Adobe Audition (*http://www.adobe.com*)
79 ACX Studio Gear (*https://blog.acx.com/2013/10/01/acx-studio-gear-series-part-3-headphones*)

RECORDING BASICS

Once you have selected the equipment, next step is learning how to use it, and how to use it well. Every setup is different, every room is different, and each person is different. There is no point giving you specific advice on how to record; however, teaching the basics is another thing.

The most important principle of recording is to get it right at the source. That is, I would say 80% of the work. When your recording sounds good 'raw'—that is without any post-production work—later fixes will be minimal. Remember, you can't polish a rock and pretend it's a diamond. The same law applies to sound recording.

In this chapter, I will give you a few helpful tips that will make production and post-editing much easier and, I hope, more enjoyable. Let's start with distance and proximity effect.

DISTANCE AND PROXIMITY EFFECT

Moving the microphone either closer or further than three inches from the lips will help. Three inches from a microphone is the distance where 'pops' are most present. With the dynamic mic[80] you can have it near your lips and still shout out loud, but with a condenser, you may want to have a bit more distance. Move the mic around, try it above or below the lips, try moving it to the side. Listen if it makes any difference at all.

A critical note is to keep the recording consistent. There is nothing worse than a recording where the voice actor goes off-mic during the sentence. It's almost impossible to fix, as not only volume will change but also the sound of the voice.

Another thing to watch out is the proximity effect. Proximity effect occurs when you place a microphone too close to a sound source, e.g. an acoustic guitar. The result will be a boomy, low-end sound, as the mic will pick up lower frequencies the most. Try to roll off low frequencies at source when it's possible; some mics have the option to do so. You can also do it on input track in your software. The easiest way to fix that is to move the microphone away from the source.

Then again, if you are in a noisy environment, such as a pub, you probably want to have the microphone as close as possible, and that's when the frequency roll off comes into play. In a comfortable environment, such as your house, you have more control. Test your microphone, listen to your recordings and select the setting that compliments your voice.

A trick that I tell my clients, especially valuable with podcasters, is to make a mark on the floor where you sit or stand for the recording and to do the same for your microphone. It will make your recordings consistent across the project. As a result, when you record half of a podcast today and half of it tomorrow, it will sound the same. I promise you that if you don't mark it, you will forget the exact positions.

POP SHIELD

What are pops? Pops are lower frequency plosive sounds, especially audible on 'p' and 'b' letters. The problem occurs when you are close to the microphone. This issue is linked to the proximity effect; a microphone will be sensitive to low-frequency air blasts, and that's what plosive sounds are.

How does a pop shield work? It breaks up the 'puff' of air, so it is no longer such a strong force, although high frequencies pass with no problem. The distance you should mount it is a couple of inches from the microphone. There needs to be a small gap of air to make the pop shield work.

Any condenser, capacitor mic will need a pop shield, these are sensitive to any turbulence. With dynamic mics, you can get away with a lot more, but by any means they are not immune to plosives. If you are working with a USB mic, the pop shield should be on the top of your list.

> *The phrase to test plosives:*
> "Peter Piper picked a peck of pickled peppers."

SIBILANCE AND PENCIL TECHNIQUE

I want to show you a technique that not many people know about; it's an old school trick that I have learnt from a veteran sound engineer. Sibilance. What is it? It's the nasty 'essses', irritating sounds that the microphone will pick up. It depends on a microphone as much as on your voice. Modern techniques would include a De-esser plugin and EQ. It helps, but don't overdo it. De-esser will compress the voice, and too much EQ will cut the presence, the 'air' of a recording. If the recording is bad, you may have to use gain to lower the 'essess', but these are all techniques for post-production. You want to control it at the source!

Everyone is different but start with a microphone placement. A pop shield won't help here, but the distance might. Stand a bit further from the microphone, test out the 'esssses'. You can also experiment with the placement; point it toward the throat and listen if that helps. Try out different scenarios.

During my studies, an old school recording engineer told me about another technique. It may seem bizarre, but try it out. Grab a pen or a pencil and tape it to the front of the microphone. Make sure it touches the grill, but don't tape over it. It should disrupt some of the air force. Does it work? Some say it does; others say it doesn't. If you are struggling to get the sound you want, there's no harm in trying.

The wrong microphone for the voice is the main culprit. Unfortunately, for most podcasting beginners, budgeting is important, and you won't be able to try a variety of microphones. These techniques should help you to get a better recording at the source.

> *The phrase to test sibilance:*
> "Sibilance, six, seven, settings."

ENVIRONMENT

Acoustics is an art of measuring space and treating it with appropriate materials. The subject of acoustics is colossal and requires years of in-depth studying and experience. Try to think about it beyond soundproofing a room. Acoustics affects every underground metro station, every shopping mall, school or office. Architects design all these buildings with acoustics in mind.

I'm not going to teach you all about acoustics in here, but I want to give you a few basic principles and tips on what you can do to improve your room.

Acoustics start with room measurement. First, you measure the size of a room and then the frequency response. You do it with a special microphone and, based on calculations, you install appropriate materials.

The other important measurement is reverberation, called RT60, which is the time it takes for sound to diminish by 60dB (near silence).

Most of these kinds of measurements are out of reach for beginners and people who want to record a podcast in their bedrooms. Before you ignore everything, just make sure you are aware of your room's shortcomings, and these are:
- *excessive reverberation* – an echo will affect your recordings; it may be a long echo in an empty hall or short echo in a small empty room.
- *unbalanced frequencies* – it happens when low frequencies are muted, and higher frequencies sound weak.
- *ringing tone* – clap your hands in a small empty room; you will hear an unpleasant ringing called the flutter echo.
- *booming bass* – affects small bedroom studios, everything sounds dull because of standing low frequencies.
- *early reflections* – bouncing reflections from nearest walls that affect your recording and listening.
- *isolation* – any unwanted external sounds.
- *standing waves* – static nodes that stay in one spot.

Quite a lot to wrap your head around. But! I say you should not worry, don't treat your room as a studio. It will never sound 'pro', as it wasn't designed to do that. Learn the limitations, and improvise.

First of all, listen to your recordings with headphones rather than loudspeakers. Good headphones will give you a direct sound, not an ideal solution but the best in your situation.

With the microphone:

- use close mic technique. The closer you are to the microphone, less noise it will capture.
- use the directionality of the microphone, so turn it away from unwanted sources.
- make a little vocal booth – do it with a duvet, blankets or cushions, put them around your microphone and it will help to isolate the sound.
- close the windows.
- shut the doors.
- switch off any noise-generating equipment such as washing machine.

There are two common choices when it comes to acoustic materials: absorbers and diffusers.[81, 82]

Absorbers will absorb unwanted sounds. Believe it or not, your bed and mattress are decent absorbers. Same with cushions and pillows, so put them near your recording space.

Diffusers break the frequencies and 'deconstruct' the force of the air. Your bookshelf, your desk; the more stuff you have in your room, the better. Unless you are going for a kind of 'bathroom' reverb sound on your voice, avoid recording in an empty room with bare walls.

If you have money, you can invest in an early reflections shield, which will help. Again, if you are thinking of professional mixing career or recording, then you will have to re-evaluate your situation. For simple podcasting, just a basic understanding of acoustics is enough, but make sure to make the best out of the situation. Watch the microphone, cover the windows and I'm sure it will turn out great.

FOOD AND DRINKS

What to eat and drink when you record? Your recording is as strong as the weakest link, and when it comes to your voice, you want it to be the strongest. You want to avoid anything that will dehydrate you; cigarettes and alcohol will have the biggest impact on your voice; black coffee or black tea can sometimes affect you too.

The other thing is food. You should avoid eating big meals before a recording session. Your body will divert energy into digestion and a microphone will pick up stomach rumble. You don't want to be hungry, as it will also cause unwanted sounds from your body. Some people say to avoid acidic foods and drinks or dairy products. Some say to eat a sour Granny Smith apple. I say, learn what works for you.

Apart from a good night's sleep, always have water ready. Room temperature is the best, as cold water will contract vocal chords. I also like to drink green tea as it soothes my throat.

Principles such as avoiding cigarettes, coffee or alcohol will help; a good night's sleep and frequent breaks are desirable. The minute you feel like you are tired and your voice may be fatigued, stop. You are not doing yourself any favours; you want to deliver the best performance. I can be quite energetic and ready to record in the morning, but with time, as I get hungry, I get irritated and lose all my enthusiasm.

I can fix it with breaks and healthy snacks throughout the session, but when I break for a large meal, it is hard for me to get back into that morning mindset. I know that, in my case, it is better to pick up the next day and spend the afternoon doing something else.

You know your body and voice better than anyone. Start recording with a plan, but don't be afraid to stop when you feel that it is not your day. Otherwise, you'll spend a few hours recording just for the sake of it, even though you know that you are not giving your best. The next day, when you listen back to it, you will hit the delete button and start again.

WHAT IF YOU HATE YOUR VOICE?

Let's paint a scene. You finished writing a perfect script, you know a thing or two about recording, you got your dream setup ready to go. Let's record the first take! Straightforward and smooth. That wasn't scary, was it? Let's now listen back to it and do a quick check... Suddenly, you hear yourself. "Oh my, do I really sound like that?!" It's harsh, whiny, nasal, monotonous, slow. You have just found out that you hate your voice.

Of course, I'm exaggerating. You probably heard yourself speak before and hated that too. So why is that? And is that how other people hear you? To answer the second question: unfortunately, yes it is. The recording shows how the rest of the world hears you every day. Why is it different to what you are used to?

To put it in the most basic terms, when you speak, not only do you receive vibrations from your mouth to your ears but also from your skin, skull, throat, bones. Your whole body reacts when you move your lips, and it affects your perception of the voice.

For many, it is a huge barrier, and if you wish to pursue a dream of starting a podcast, you will need to learn to love your voice. First and foremost, record yourself as often as you can, and play it back! At some point, you will get used to hearing yourself and it will stop bothering you. Make it a daily habit—record, listen back to it, delete. Do a quick read out of every script you write moments after the first draft is done. That leads to the following advice: learn how to improve your voice.

You can control your pitch, speed, emphasis and presence. When you listen back to your voice, don't think in terms of how much you don't like it. Listen and take notes. What can you change? How can you improve your diction, your pronunciation? Change the pitch once in a while to break out the monotony.

Also, recognise what you like about your voice. Ask other people what they like and don't like about your voice. Improve on weaknesses, but focus on the strengths. I know it may sound a bit narcissistic and shallow, but learn to love your voice, and get used to hearing it.

Check the first few episodes of *Casefile* and then listen to the latest one. The improvement in Host's narration is colossal, but that came with time and practice. He still says that he hates his voice, though!

A FEW OTHER TIPS

Before I close up the chapter, I want to give you some quick tips on sound recording. I know that it is a lot of information but, if you want your podcast to thrive, you need to perfect the tools.

Understand your recording
What do you want to record?
What equipment do you have?
Where are you going to record and when?
Planning is your first step; the worst thing to do is to improvise on the spot.

Start at the source
Correct mic placement is a must and watch input levels as you record.

Use small number of microphones
It probably won't be a problem for you, but when the number of microphones doubles, there is a potential acoustic gain decrease by 3dB, meaning that you have to turn down the input of every additional microphone to avoid feedback. It's quite tricky when you have to set up a large band on stage.

Use shock mounts where possible
Especially with condensers, shock mounts will limit vibrations and low-frequency bumps in the recording.

Keep audio cables away from power cables
They will induce unwanted noise and interference.

Switch off your phone!
Interference and distraction, you don't need it.

3-1 rule is a rule of thumb
It means that if you are using two microphones the distance between them should be three times bigger than the distance from the microphones to the source. It will reduce phasing, also known as comb filtering, where frequencies cancel each other out because of a delay in the sound.

Use polar patterns to omit unwanted sounds
Keep microphones away from loudspeakers to avoid feedback. Use headphones to monitor your recordings.

Run a test recording and listen back to it

Always record more than you need
If you are in the zone, do your whole recording in one sitting. But if you are not sure about the style of delivery, record another take. It is much easier to do that than to set it all up again for one retake.

Experiment!
Try different placement, settings, rooms, blankets and whatever you wish. You may prefer to stand up or sit down, record at night or in the morning. Particularly in the beginning, it is important to learn the basics, but it is also crucial to have fun with as many different options as you can!

Record yourself all the time [83]
Make notes on what works and what doesn't and don't try to make it perfect the first time. Let your friends or family members listen to your podcasts and register what they say.

All feedback is necessary
When I work with clients and clean or edit their recordings, I always advise and ask about the setup. You wouldn't believe how a simple tip of just standing in one position or changing microphone placement can help.

The microphone is your friend; it makes you audible to the whole world. Don't overlook it; learn it, test it, make sure you know it better than anyone. It will take some time, but I guarantee you will be glad that you made the effort.

---

80 Shure SM7B (*https://www.shure.co.uk/products/microphones/sm7b*)
81 The Acoustic Treatment Guide for Panels & Foam (*https://ledgernote.com/columns/studio-recording/acoustic-treatment-guide-for-panels-and-foam*)
82 The Ultimate Guide to Acoustic Treatment for Home Studios (*http://ehomerecordingstudio.com/acoustic-treatment-101*)
83 Quick Time (*https://support.apple.com/en-gb/HT201175*)

EDITING, MIXING AND MASTERING

Recording your podcast is the first step. Like with any other entertainment product, be it a movie, a song or any show, there are always three stages: pre-production, production and post-production. So far I covered the first two, now let's focus on the last one: post-production.

In post-production for podcasts, you have editing, mixing and mastering, and at the end the exporting and naming. You will do the tasks in a sequence. Depending on the show, the post-production stage can either be simple and easy or time-consuming and ambitious. Let's take *Casefile* as an example.

With a show like that, the pre-production takes most of the time; that's when we do the research, script writing and editing. Post-production is for sound editing, scoring, mixing and mastering. The production stage is not that difficult, nor time-consuming in comparison to the other two. By production, I mean the actual recording of the narration by the Host.

Although, if you are planning an interview-style podcast, pre-production and actual recording are where you will focus, as mixing it all together afterwards should not be that big of a problem. When I help out with those kinds of shows, I usually do a simple edit to take out mistakes and apply a few global audio processes to clean up the recording. I add intro and outro and make sure it all sounds even and clear. An hour of interview-style podcast takes me around three hours to edit, mix and master. To compare, an hour of *Casefile* takes three to five days in post-production. That means editing, scoring, mixing and mastering.

As you can see, there is a reason why *Casefile* sounds good and keeps attracting a large audience. There is a lot of work involved.

In this chapter, I want to give you an overview of each post-production step as well as a few tips on how you can make it as efficient as possible.

EDITING

Audio editing is a laborious task of making noisy and lousy recordings sound good. It is one of the processes that makes the project whole and prepares the session for mixing.

See it as writing a book. You create a draft and then spend time editing out the mistakes and extraneous material, polishing it into the final product. Sound editing is not just cleaning up bad recordings; a few creative processes are easier to do during editing, before the audio moves onto the next stage. In podcasting and voice editing you won't have to worry about them too much, though.

Tools

Picking software is essential, and there are a few important things to consider in your selection.

Stability, speed and control

Stability is self-explanatory. The less system crashes you get, the less chamomile tea you need to drink. The knowledge that you can rely on the system goes a long way, especially if you want to release your podcast in the next few days.

The speed is vital, as in how fast you can edit and what the responsiveness of the program is. System lag is the curse of every editor. There are a lot of variables that go into the equation, but some workstations are quicker to react than others.

Control over the interface is last on the list. Some programs try to be helpful and offer an array of smart, all-in-one functions. They are useful, but when it comes to fast-paced editing, a clear list of keyboard shortcuts and the ability to make easy customisations are on the top of the pyramid.

Ground work

What sort of recording will you work on? How much time do you have? These are the most fundamental questions you need to ask before commencing the work.

Isolate sounds into groups, like dialogue, effects and music, and create a basic structure. Arrangements, like colour-coding, naming conventions and general order of audio files, will make the process smoother. It is easy to get lost when there are thousands of sounds to get through.

Techniques

When it comes to editing techniques, it's all about cutting up, cleaning and moving sounds around.

Cleaning unwanted noises, such as lip smacks, clicks or cloth movement is tiresome and not every recording will be easy to fix. There are special tools, such as Izotope Rx,[84] that will help you to automate some of these tasks, but I will get to them in the advanced editing section.

Cutting up and moving sounds around is simple, as it only requires the most basic functions of your software.

Always have a backup of the original sound. I always have two tracks in my session, one called ORG_DIAL, which is a 'raw' recording and the other one called DIAL, that is edited dialogue with all the applied processing.

Completion

On big productions, an editor must work to strict guidelines, such as file formats, naming conventions and colour-coding. When I worked as a sound editor on movies, file management was always a top priority. Moving audio assets between different departments, and often countries, on a daily basis, required attention to detail that has stayed with me ever since.

So, even if you are a one-person band and are planning on doing everything by yourself, having a clean session and working on templates will make your life much easier.

#Editing Casefile

After the Host records an episode, I receive the script and the GarageBand session with his narration. He puts together a rough structure, selecting the takes and placing everything in order, clips from archives included.

I will listen to the episode and do the first edit. This is what you will have to do if you are doing any podcast.

I will move the narration around, making the gaps between the sentences longer or shorter. It depends on what kind of emotional impact I'm looking for: a long pause for a dramatic scene, short pauses for intense moments. I will also get rid of any mistakes, unnecessary breaths, mouth noises and general background noise. It's a simple process but necessary if you wish your podcast to sound professional.

For an hour of recorded narration, it can take me around two hours to do the editing; it depends on the state of the recording.

Advanced editing

Advanced editing requires professional tools as well as deeper technical knowledge about audio. To get to a proficient level, not only have I studied audio engineering and worked on multiple projects, but I have also honed the craft during my years as a sound editor at a movie studio. I worked on big projects for Disney, Pixar and Marvel, among many others, and hence I had technical experience when I took on producing *Casefile*.

Of course, I still learnt a tonne and continued to develop my skills with each episode, but I want you to know that it takes time, practice and a lot of studying to get to a professional level of audio editing.

When you start out, don't worry about it too much, the most important thing is to take the first step and to create the first podcast. You can worry about polishing the production after you decide to get serious about your show.

It was the same with *Casefile*. The Host produced the first few episodes by himself; he didn't plan to make anything out of it. When the podcast started to gain traction, he realised he needed help with audio editing, and so he hired me.

Advanced editing techniques include global processes, such as de-noising, cleaning up the dialogue and fixing up smaller mistakes. It takes a lot of time and work, so unless you have a huge audience and your podcasts are reviewed on a daily basis, don't worry about it too much. However, do keep it at the back of your mind.

#*Casefile advanced editing*
Once my first edit in Pro Tools[85] is complete, I send it to Izotope Rx plugin. These tools are expensive (around $1,500) but are the industry standard for audio restoration and fixing dialogue. I start the process by applying global modules.

First, I cut everything below 65 Hz; unfortunately, the Host still records in his bedroom, and as much as he has improved the acoustics, there is still a lot of rumble going on in the background, so I get rid of it.

The next step is cleaning up the narration as a whole. I apply the De-Click module that gets rid of more prominent mouth noises; I run the De-Plosive module that minimises plosive sounds on 'p' and 'b' letters.

Finally, I apply the Dialogue De-Noise module twice, first with higher setting and second pass on lower option. It takes a few minutes to exercise these global processes, depending on the length of the narration. Now the fun starts!

I listen to the recording once again, fixing any other mistakes 'on-the-fly' with Izotope Rx. I get rid of unnecessary breaths, clicks, mouth noises and other imperfections. I use a selection of tools, such as Spectral Repair's Attenuation, Replace and Ambience Match. This process is long and tedious; depending on the recording, it can take a few solid hours. After that, I send the file back to Pro Tools software.

MUSIC AND INTRO

Music is central to *Casefile*. It helps to create the atmosphere and tension and supports the excellent narration of the Host. Not every podcast needs that kind of scoring and, to be honest, few require it. If you are planning on starting an audio drama, then music will be on your mind, but if you want to run a talk show, then besides a catchy intro and maybe a few sound effects, you won't need to worry about much else.

With the music, you can buy themes from libraries such as AudioJungle,[86]

Pond5[87] or Audioblocks.[88] There are plenty of sites like that, just search for 'royalty free music'. You can also hire a composer to create a bespoke score. Those two options are very different and require—as you can imagine—a different level of funding. Royalty-free music will be easy on your wallet, but hiring a music composer can cost from a few hundred to thousands of dollars per episode. So yes, it is expensive to run a show like *Casefile*.

My advice would be to either go with royalty-free music in the beginning or hire an aspiring composer, a friend who can do the work for 'mate's rates.' If he or she is still learning, you both can grow your show into something special, and with time re-negotiate the compensation. Royalty-free music is the easiest method, but you can end up using cues that other people have used before thus losing out on originality.

With the intro, it's a bit different. You need something catchy, something that will introduce the show with each episode. For *Casefile*, we tried to come up with another intro, to change it up, to make it original. In the end, we decided to stay with the old one, even though it was from a royalty-free music library and was possibly used by other people. Don't try to be original just for the sake of it; it is much better to stay faithful and authentic with your goals.

Besides the intro, you may also want a short theme music. As you noticed, with *Casefile* it goes: Sponsors/Ads – Intro Sound Effect – Intro Narration – Theme Music – Main Episode (ads in the middle) – Theme Music. Even without a bespoke soundtrack, we would still need an intro sound effect (the heartbeat and flatline sounds) and theme music. For your show, you will at least need these two to buy/create.

#*Casefile scoring*

Casefile has a strange process when it comes to music. We have a standard ads section at the front, we play a quiet underneath score for the sponsors, then we start the episode with a flatline/heartbeat sound effect that doesn't change. The Host narrates the intro of the episode and then the theme music kicks in. We also play it at the end of the podcast.

The originality of *Casefile* lies in its bespoke score. We have two composers who work on each episode, I do around 60% of the score, and Andrew Joslyn[89] does the rest. The way it works is when I read the script and edit the narration, I create musical cues for each scene. These cues will range from two to sometimes ten-minute sections. I make a note of it all and send the edited dialogue to Andrew, who then works on his score.

I start working on my score straight away. I use a couple of software instruments, such as Spectrasonics[90] Omnisphere, Keyscape, Trilian and Spitfire Virtual Instruments.[91] I write original music wherever I can and, for some parts, I re-mix cues from older episodes. I always try to have a central motif going through the episode and to give each character their own sound. It's both a hard and a rewarding process, given the fact that on average the episodes are an hour long and sometimes up to two hours!

After a few days, I receive cues from Andrew and proceed to the next stage, which is mixing.

MIXING

Sound mixing is an art of combining many sounds into one, and there is a simple metaphor to describe mixing. A lot of mixers say it is like cooking; you add different ingredients to create the perfect dish. Add too much, or too little of something and your mix is not as tasty as you wanted it to be.

The reason sound mixing is a respectable skill is that it requires a lot of technical knowledge. Also good hearing, subtle touch, creative mind and, of course, a lot of experience. A good mix of your podcast is not going to need that much dedication, but it is important to have the fundamental knowledge of the craft.

Tools

The days of analogue mixing are pretty much gone. There are still people who will fight for it, but the world has gone digital, and the art of mixing sound followed. Your basic tools for mixing will be a good computer, software of your choice and maybe a surface control that acts as a mixing desk.

The surface control will not affect the sound, as all the processing happens inside the software. Sets of faders and knobs correspond to the interface and make the process much easier than working with a mouse and keyboard.

Remember, the most important tools are your hands and your ears. Well, your eyes too, as a lot of work happen on the computer screen.

Groundwork
Preparation is everything. To do a good job, make sure you label everything and keep it on the same audio tracks. Keep intro sound effects on one track, music theme on another, voice number one, voice number two and so on. I also use colour-coding to keep my session organised; each element has a different appearance, which helps to speed up the process. Another thing is plugins.

For mixing, you will be using EQ and compression, maybe a bit of reverb. The best way to work is to save your session as a template so you can use it for future podcasts. With time, as you learn more about the specifics of your show, you can improve your template and customise it to your liking.

Techniques
Methods of mixing are a topic for a large book, and everyone has their opinion on the subject, but it is important to understand the fundamentals. Volume, panning, EQ, and compression are your essential tools when it comes to mixing.

Volume Control
You will have to decide which sounds will take priority over the others. Loud action scenes are awesome, but sometimes a moment of silence can have an even bigger impact.

Panning
Stands for a panorama, and it means locating the sounds around you. 'Pan it to the left or right' means moving the sound around the spectrum.

EQ
Represents equalisation, and is a sound frequency tool. Each sound has a frequency spectrum that you can adjust to your liking. Does your voice have too much low end? You can cut it out from its spectrum and create space for other sounds.

Compression

Makes loud sounds quiet and evens out the mix. It is the most valuable tool when it comes to controlling the dynamics of your mix. It can take years before you grasp the value of compression.

Printing

To print your mix means to record it into stems and master tracks. A stereo master will have two audio tracks – left and right. A mono master will only have one track: centre.

Besides printing your full mix, it is important to record stems, such as music, voice one, voice two, intro. Stems are your mix elements but combined into single audio tracks. For example, all your royalty music can be printed as a 'music bed', one audio track. It helps to simplify the session for the final touches and mastering.

To mix a podcast is to make it sound as good as possible, to make it clear and even, to get rid of unwanted frequencies. When you record an interview, you will want your sponsor's ad, intro, and the dialogue to have a similar, constant volume. You will use a combination of volume gain and compression to get all your recordings into shape.

EQ will help you to 'make room' for the sounds by cutting or boosting frequencies. For example, low frequencies will be a problem, especially if you record in your bedroom. With EQ you can cut off anything below the threshold of your voice. You will remove unwanted 'bass' but keep your voice sounding natural. Before starting on your mix, I would recommend to either watch a tutorial or read a book on compression and EQ, to learn basic functions and techniques.

A mix can make or break your podcast, especially if you insist on having music underneath your voice. Otherwise, I guarantee that the music will overshadow the narration and you will get complaints from your listeners.

#Casefile mixing

Casefile is almost a weekly show, and even when we have a break, I still work on future episodes. With original content and music being produced each week, I had to make the process of mixing as efficient as possible.

During music composing, I record musical elements on separate tracks and do a preliminary mix on the go. After that, I bounce the music intro a stereo track – a music bed. I then listen to the episode and mix it 'on-the-fly'. I use clip gain function in Pro Tools as well as mixing plugins from Izotope, Alloy 2[93] & Neutron. I usually do two passes for the mix, first one to get the levels right and then on the next day I sit down with fresh ears and listen to the episode once again, correcting any issues that I might have missed.

For the narration, I use Neutron as well as Alloy 2 to get the best sound possible. I work on templates; therefore, I don't need to set up my session for each episode.

NOVEMBER 2019 UPDATE

As Izotope discontinued Alloy plugins I now solely use Neutron for mixing with a little help from Izotope Nectar plugin.

Listening

With mixing comes listening, and critical listening is the key to a perfect podcast. I want to share with you a few tips on listening, most of them are more applicable for mixing music or movies, but I always treat my work on podcasts in the same way as I would for a full feature film. Apply the principles, and you will end up with a great product.

Look at the big picture

Perfectionism is not an asset, and you should throw it away. It is so easy to get caught up in details and record the same line over and over again. 'If it sounds good, then it's good' is the saying, so, in the words of Princess Elsa, let it go and move on!

Listen in balance
Listen to the narration with the music. If you are recording a script, listen to the whole of it rather than just a few words. You would be amazed how forgiving listeners are and how quickly they adapt to the noise floor, as long as it is consistent.

Watch the screen
Mixing is all about listening, but tracking the screen helps. How do the waveforms look? What about the sound meters? Monitor with your eyes and ears.

Work on headphones but listen on different systems
Reference your mix on laptop speakers, on cheap USB computer loudspeakers, on cheap ear-ins, on expensive monitors. People listen to podcasts on different settings so check it on as many as you can.

Listen in various environments
Go outside and listen to it, listen in your car, take a phone with you and listen on a train, when you walk down the road, at the gym. That's how people consume podcasts so make sure yours sounds amazing in 'noisy' places.

Turn the volume down
If you turn the volume down, are the words still audible? When it all sounds good on a low level, it's a good sign.

Close your eyes and listen back to the mix
Focus on details and let go of distractions.

Have a reference material ready nearby, another podcast or audio drama
Listen to it and compare it with your own mix. Does it sound the same or better?

Give someone else to listen
Another pair of ears is a great help. You may be stressing about something the listeners don't even notice.

Fresh ears

Listening to the same recording for hours won't help. On the contrary, your ears will give in to fatigue; it will affect the balance and volume of the mix. Give it a rest and listen to it the next morning. I also take a five-ten minute break every half hour of work. Make tea, read something, go outside. When you are working on closed-cup headphones, your ears will get tired quickly.

#Casefile listening

For my main work, I use Sony MDR-7506[94] headphones, as I do editing and mixing on them. I also use Adam A5X monitors[95] to reference the mix from time to time, but the crucial part is listening to it on cheap ear-in headphones. Over 80% of podcast listening happens on mobile phones and, without exaggerating, most people listen on cheap headphones that come with their smartphones.

I have five pairs of ear-ins, different brands. I will test and listen to the mix on each one of them, and I try to make it sound as good as possible on each one. It is often a Herculean task, almost impossible, but I try to get better each time.

Apart from that, I take short breaks every thirty minutes. When you listen on headphones for too long, your ears give in to fatigue and stop noticing details. Your hearing gets used to the noise and small volume changes.

NOVEMBER 2019 UPDATE

As I mentioned before, I've upgraded my gear and now use the Sony MDR-7506 headphones just for editing and replaced it with AKG K712 Pro headphones for mixing and mastering.

MASTERING

Mastering is the last process in post-production and the most nuanced one. It's the last action before exporting your podcast as an MP3 file. During mastering, you take the whole mix and make it louder by applying additional EQ and compression to the final track. Mastering is a delicate process, especially when it comes to music mastering.

For your podcast, what you will need to do during the mastering process is to make it louder and even out the dynamics. Podcasting platforms don't have strict rules when it comes to volume, but a general rule is not to compress the sound too much and to keep a bit of dynamic range, especially if you want to master an audio drama.

I read somewhere that for mono files you should keep around –19 dB LUFS and for stereo –16d B LUFS. I tend to keep my mixes around 19dB, and I carefully watch the dynamic range. I guess it depends on your goals. If it's just a simple interview-style podcast, then loudness will be your priority. You will want the voices to be clear and audible to the listener.

If you are looking at starting something similar to *Casefile*, then approach it similarly to a movie mix. Dynamic range and subtle touches will be substantial for the listeners who like to hear your show in the evening with their headphones on.

Don't skip mastering: use simple limiting and EQ to push your mix before exporting it as a final audio file. It will make your podcast stand above other shows.

#*Casefile mastering*

My setup is quite unusual. I use Izotope Ozone 7[96] for my mastering, which is, in my opinion, one of the best solutions for audio. I keep both Ozone 7 and Insight, a metering plugin on my master track, for most of my work. Once my mix is done, I do the final touches in the same session.

I operate on templates, so most of it is automated, and when I'm happy with the sound, I bounce the track into the 'offline' mode to a stereo track. Within Ozone 7 I use Equalizer, Vintage Limiter, Dynamics Multiband Compression and Maximizer modules to give the show a crisp and natural sound.

The narration is still being recorded in the bedroom, so I try to reduce the 'room' sound as much as I can as well as control mid-frequencies that make the sounds 'muddy.'

> **NOVEMBER 2019 UPDATE**
>
> I still use Izotope Ozone plugins for mastering, but the last version, which is Ozone 9 Advanced. It offers more options and insights for mastering.

EXPORTING YOUR PODCAST

Once you are happy with your mix, it's time to export your podcast as a final audio file. In Pro Tools, and probably most audio sequencers, you will have an option to 'bounce' your mix offline or in real-time, as well as choose the format.

Bouncing is combining all the elements of your podcast into a single mono or stereo track. Real-time bouncing is called 'printing' and, as you probably guessed, takes the time of your podcast to complete the task. So, if your episode is forty minutes long, then the bounce will take forty minutes. Depending on the way of printing you can also listen back to your final mix and stop it during the process. Offline bouncing is much faster, and it only takes a few minutes. You won't be hearing anything, but you can cancel the process if you wish.

In the past, offline bouncing was frowned upon as it could induce audio errors to the mix. However, today I wouldn't worry about it. I always use offline bouncing, given the fact that most of the *Casefile* episodes are over an hour long!

Format

You can choose if your podcast will be a mono or stereo file. Mono is one signal that sits in the centre, so, for example, your voice. Stereo is two signals, one panned to the left and the other to the right. Which one should you choose? If you are running a simple podcast, a talk show, then go with mono as it will have half the size of a stereo file.

The things to watch out for are your intro sound effects and theme music, which will more than likely be stereo files. You will have to bounce them down as mono files and check if they still sound okay. You will pay for the hosting space, so it makes sense to keep the files as small as possible, especially in the beginning.

I would recommend going stereo once your podcast is growing, or if you are using a soundtrack throughout your show. Music in mono sounds boring, and it's a pain to bounce it down to mono every time. You can listen to old *Casefile* episodes and compare them to new ones to hear the difference between mono and stereo mix.

> **NOVEMBER 2019 UPDATE**
>
> After re-mastering the early *Casefile* episodes, all of the content is now in stereo. I would advise forgetting about mono files and focus on stereo bouncing, considering that everyone is using at least some music in their podcasts.

Audio quality and MP3 files

Another thing to consider while exporting your podcast is choosing the correct quality settings. Most programs will allow you to export uncompressed audio and MP3 files.

With podcasts it is all about the size, not only because of the hosting costs but also the storage space on mobiles. Most users download podcasts to their phones and at the moment size still matters, albeit less and less each year.

I'm all about sound quality, and especially with *Casefile* I take pride to make it sound as good as possible. Skimping on size would mean inferior quality.

Let me show you some numbers.

'Case 44, Peter Falconio' was almost two hours long. Uncompressed file. wav was 2.01GB in size, impossible to host and download for most people.

- MP3 file with 192Kbps quality was 166.7MB
- MP3 file with 320Kbps quality was 278.3MB

For an audio drama such as *Casefile*, I wouldn't go below 192Kbps as you will start to hear the difference below that threshold. With an interview-style podcast, Skype recordings or live talk, going down to and even below 128Kbps is acceptable. Some people suggest 64Kbps to keep the size to a minimum, however, I would not recommend it.

Podcasting is all about the audio, so if you skimp on quality, there is nothing else to cover these issues.

#*Casefile exporting*

I tend to go with the highest quality possible; I'm often on the fence between 192Kbps and 320Kbps as the difference in quality is minimal but substantial in size. When we release longer episodes, such as Case 44, Peter Falconio, we tend to get a few complaints about the size of the file. As you noticed there is a difference of over 100MB and the episode was released as 320Kbps MP3.

But I think about the future; in years to come, mobile phones will have more storage built in. Therefore, the size of the podcast won't matter as much. Old episodes will hopefully still be available for the new fans, and I want them to experience *Casefile* in the best quality that was possible at the time of release.

Of course, I would prefer to have the episodes up as uncompressed files. However, that will not be available for at least some time. The neutral and the most decent option is still 192Kbps.

Another thing altogether is bandwidth cost, but I'll talk about it in the chapter on hosting.

File naming and metadata

It is safe to say that consistency is the key to everything. When you start your podcast, it is desirable to choose a naming convention and stick to it. It will look right on your home page, and you avoid confusion with the listeners. If you decide to change the naming after a few episodes, don't worry too much as you can still do it on your hosting service, but it takes a couple of days to update.

You should pay attention to metadata, though. Metadata is data that describes other data. Another description of your podcast, with things like date of creation, what kind of file it is, a category.

You can either use your software of choice to add the naming and description during the export of your podcast, or you can adjust it later on, especially if you want to add a thumbnail.

Naming and metadata will also make your podcasts easier to discover, so don't skip that step!

#Casefile naming

I export the files without proper naming, just something alongside case44_final. I then use Apple iTunes[97] to add naming and metadata. I open the exported MP3 file in iTunes and then click on the 'Get info' option next to the name. First, I go into the Options tab and change media kind to Podcast.

I move onto Details tab, type in the case name under the title, '*Casefile*' under author, the case number under podcast and True Crime in a genre box. I also change the artwork to small thumbnails with the episode's name. I then need to look for the file in the iTunes Music folder, as iTunes will make a copy of your podcast. I change the name of the file before uploading it to servers.

Casefile follows the same naming for all the episodes:

Case number: Case name

Case 44: Peter Falconio

---

84 Izotope Rx (*https://www.izotope.com/en/products/repair-and-edit/rx.html*)
85 Pro Tools (*n 72*)
86 Audio Jungle (*https://audiojungle.net*)
87 Pond5 (*https://www.pond5.com/royalty-free-music*)
88 Audioblocks (*https://www.audioblocks.com*)
89 Andrew Joslyn Music (*n 3*)
90 Spectrasonics (*https://www.spectrasonics.net/products/omnisphere*)
91 Spitfire (*https://www.spitfireaudio.com*)
92 Alloy 2 (*https://www.izotope.com/en/products/mix/alloy.html*)
93 Sony MDR7506 (*http://www.sony.co.uk/pro/product/broadcast-products-professional-audio-headphones/mdr-7506/overview*)
94 Adam (*https://www.adam-audio.com/en/ax-series/a5x*)
95 Ozone (*https://www.izotope.com/en/products/master-and-deliver/ozone.html*)
96 Insight (*https://www.izotope.com/en/products/mix/insight.html*)
97 iTunes (*n 5*)

HOSTING

What is hosting? Hosting is a remote server where you upload podcasts. People will download/listen to your show from that location, and you need it to store the files. It is the same as with websites; you host the site on remote servers that guarantee upkeep time and security, among other functions. They also handle all the traffic to your site.

When we started working on *Casefile*, we didn't know much about podcasting or hosting and had to learn it as we went along. Unfortunately, it didn't go as smoothly as we planned and we had to change hosting a few times. With each transfer, we had some problems, which I will describe at the end of this chapter.

As you can imagine, hosting costs can range from few dollars to thousands, depending on the traffic and downloads of your show. With the show like *Casefile*, there is a lot of traffic to handle. In your case—as you are just starting out—the costs will be minimal. However, I would recommend doing proper research and choosing the right hosting from the beginning. It will save you headaches down the road, and if the show gains popularity, you can always negotiate a 'special' deal with your hosting providers.

I will describe a few providers that we have used in the past, and offer some pros and cons for each service. I hope to give you an overview of how it all looks and what to expect when you decide to go with one of the companies. The list is not comprehensive; there are a lot of options out there. Remember, choosing the right host is crucial. You don't want to find out from Twitter[98] that your podcast is not playing or can't be accessed.

RSS

RSS[99] stands for Rich Site Summary, and it's a way to send information about updated content throughout the web. Each time we upload a new episode, our RSS is updated with new information. The best way to explain it is to think about all the podcasting apps.

With Apple OS or iOS,[100] it is quite straightforward: they provide you with iTunes and a podcasting app, but with Android[101] it is a different story. When you access the Google Play Store, you will see different podcasting apps, and *Casefile* is available on all of them. Does that mean that the show is hosted on each of the podcasting apps? No, *Casefile* is still hosted on external servers. However, the RSS feed is sent from the server, letting all the podcasting apps know that a new episode is ready to stream or download. The apps process the information and display the latest *Casefile* on their feeds, and the listeners get the notification to access the content.

Another way to listen to the show is to play it with a native player, which is a direct method. We use the player when we post episodes on the website.

As you can see, correct RSS is crucial as it notifies many podcasting apps at once. Recently, we had an issue when some listeners messaged us that they couldn't access the latest episodes of *Casefile*. For a while, we were dumbfounded, as we haven't changed anything with the hosting and there was no reason for RSS to break – that was the exact message.

It turned out that some podcasting apps were still using the RSS from the SoundCloud account, where we were uploading episodes from time to time. At the beginning of 2017, we decided to delete the SoundCloud[102] account. By removing the account and not re-directing the RSS, we broke the connection with some of the podcasting apps. Thankfully, we asked the listeners to let us know which apps were not responding and then, one by one, I emailed the support with a request to change the *Casefile* RSS feed to the correct one.

As you can see, issues can come up every day, especially if you don't know everything about podcasting, when you are still learning. The good thing is that, by reading this guide, you can learn from our mistakes, which will save you a lot of time.

Now, I want to list a few hosting options for you to start your inquiry. As

I mentioned before, there are lots of alternative platforms out there so do your diligent research before you commit to one.

BLUBRRY

The company offers an all-in-one podcasting solution, with media hosting, site creation and sponsorships. We hosted *Casefile* with Blubrry[103] at the very beginning of the show.

The difference in their hosting is that they keep the files on the website as media, though there is an option for a FTP server, but only on a professional level. They guarantee unlimited bandwidth, and if you are just starting out, it could work well for your podcast. Also, if downloads are not substantial, then you shouldn't have any issues with the service. However, if you are looking at producing long-form audio dramas with a considerable size to your audio files, then it could pose a problem, especially when downloads pick up.

It's best to give them a call or write to their support and ask more details. We switched from Blubrry halfway through 2016, when our downloads were still in tens of thousands per month. It was a lot, but not enough to test their bandwidth.

SOUNDCLOUD

For the past year, we also hosted the show with SoundCloud. What we did, though, was host the show on both SoundCloud and other services! I told you we were making plenty of mistakes.

SoundCloud—especially the standard option—provides you with a cheap and easy solution. However, they lack in-depth statistics about downloads. There is a Pro Service option that offers that but we haven't tested it. We deleted the SoundCloud account as it brought a small number of downloads for each episode and we experienced an unresponsive server on their end on several occasions.

We needed a more reliable provider and didn't want to upload episodes in two places every time, but as I mentioned before, we still made a mistake and didn't redirect the SoundCloud feed, so some apps were reporting a 'Broken RSS Feed'.

ART19

ART19[104] is a new solution for podcasters, a start-up hosting company that wants to revolutionise advertising on podcasts. Their service allows for geo-targeting with ads as well as campaigns based on impressions. In theory, on the same episode, you could have an ad that is directed at Australian listeners and another one directed only at an American audience. You can also switch on and off the adverts and add the ads to old episodes, which could make it quite attractive to sponsors in the future.

LIBSYN[105]

They host big names, such as *Entrepreneur on Fire*, *Tim Ferris Show*, Pat Flynn's podcast.

They host the files on their FTP servers; they offer help with advertisers and services, such as paid premium content. They have their podcasting player and distribute the RSS throughout the web.

There are other solutions you can look at, such as PodBean[106] or Buzzsprout,[107] Audioboom,[108] however, I haven't tested them, and I can't give you an honest opinion. My experiences with hosting *Casefile* are of course biased, and you should treat them as such. Do your research, contact the support and compare different options before signing up for a service.

There are 'horror' stories on some hosting providers holding the RSS hostage during migration, which ended with them losing all the subscribers for their podcast. I don't know if the stories are true, but it's better to be safe than sorry.

> **NOVEMBER 2019 UPDATE**
>
> For the last two years, *Casefile* has been hosted by Audioboom and we will be staying with the company for the foreseeable future. They offer podcast hosting, analytics and ad sales.

COST OF HOSTING

Let's now compare the cost of hosting.

Blubrry

Blubrry offers Web Upload hosting starting at $12/month with 100MB storage and options going up to $80/month with 1,000MB storage; it is still Web Upload.

They have a 'Professional' option for commercial podcasts and host these shows on FTP server. A rate for that kind of hosting is based on both bandwidth and storage. So, both how big the size of the file is and how many people download it.

The costs are around $0.09/GB between 5–10 TB of bandwidth a month, and negotiable if you require more bandwidth than that. There are calculators for that if you want to check how much you could be paying, Google 'podcast bandwidth calculator'.

SoundCloud

SoundCloud offers free hosting service for beginners and Pro options for $10 and $20 per month. With Pro options you get additional stats as well as upload time—unlimited for the most expensive option.

Libsyn

Libsyn services start at $5/month up to $75/month with an option of the LibsynPro service for bigger podcasts, which is paid based on bandwidth. The differences between Classic and Advanced options are in monthly storage, statistics as well as transcoding.

PodBean

PodBean starts at $3 up to $99/month. Same as the others: the more you pay, the bigger storage you get, as well as other perks such as advanced statistics and the option of adding extra admins.

Buzzsprout

Buzzsprout starts free, with options up to $24/month. You pay extra for upload time, and with each plan, you get 250 GB of bandwidth. The moment your podcast goes above the numbers, they switch you to Pro plan with 1 TB of bandwidth. If you need more than that, the price is $0.15/gigabyte.

ART19

ART19 charges on bandwidth and storage, similar to Libsyn Pro and Blubrry Pro.

SUBMITTING YOUR RSS

Once you have created a podcast, you will need to submit the RSS feed to iTunes, Stitcher[109] and other apps. First of all, find out with your hosting provider how and where they send the RSS, but iTunes RSS validation is something you need to do nevertheless.

To submit the RSS, you will need graphic artwork, podcast name, at least one episode and category. I will talk about artwork specifications in the next chapter, so for now, create an Apple ID and log into iTunes Connect.[110]

With Stitcher, you will need to register as a Content Provider and submit your show's RSS. With other podcasting apps, the best way is to check if they are receiving the RSS and displaying your show. If not, contact them directly with the details. You will also need to check if your feed is correct.

It is called RSS validation, and you can do it by either Googling 'RSS validator' or using a website such as Case Feed Validator.[111] It will show you how podcasting apps view the RSS and if they see your latest uploads. It may take a few days for iTunes and Stitcher to validate your feed, so don't worry, and wait for the notification email. If you don't get it after a week, contact support for more information.

NOVEMBER 2019 UPDATE

The landscape has changed and Spotify[112] has also thrown its hat into the ring. There are now plenty of podcasting apps, so it is important to check if your hosting provider supports them all and makes it easy to send the RSS signal out everywhere.

---

98 Twitter (*n 39*)
99 RSS (*http://www.whatisrss.com*)
100 Apple (*n 73*)
101 Android (*https://www.android.com*)
102 SoundCloud (*https://soundcloud.com/for/podcasting*)
103 Blubrry (*https://www.blubrry.com*)
104 ART19 (*https://art19.com*)
105 Libsyn (*n 27*)
106 PodBean (*https://www.podbean.com*)
107 Buzzsprout (*https://www.buzzsprout.com*)
108 Audioboom (*https://audioboom.com*)
109 Stitcher (*http://www.stitcher.com/content-providers*)
110 iTunes Connect (*https://itunesconnect.apple.com*)
111 Case Feed Validator (*http://www.castfeedvalidator.com*)
112 Spotify (*https://www.spotify.com*)

ARTWORK DESIGN

There is no doubt that people are visual creatures. If beauty lies in the eye of a beholder, then most of us can recognise good design from a bad one. Podcasts are not different; yes, they are audio first, but more than often how you choose new shows is by looking at top charts and clicking the one that looks good. Your podcast's artwork needs to be attractive, have a clear message and be kind on the eyes.

With *Casefile* we went through a few changes as we grew and improved the show, and the design was one of them. When we decided to modify the logo and main artwork, we had not only been asked to provide new graphics for an iTunes feature but also wanted to have something that would be an invite to all true crime fans. Luckily, my wife and partner-in-crime, Paulina, is an excellent graphic designer and helped us to get top-quality artwork for a 'family and friends' fee. No doubt that I still owe her for all the help she provided, and still does to this day.

Another thing is that, without artwork, your RSS will not be accepted into iTunes, and as most of the listens still come through Apple's platform, I don't need to tell you that it is rather important to have good graphic assets for your show.

I know that not everyone lives with a professional designer under one roof. I want to help you to find one, though, and also give you the specifications for the artwork you need to obtain.

Apple is strict about following the guidelines, but other services such as Facebook or Twitter also require banners and logos. Not to mention the fact that it is nice to have a thumbnail to go with your metadata, as well as a particular graphic for each episode that you post on a website. Let's start with finding someone that could help you.

First of all, think if you know someone who could assist you with the design. A family member? A friend? You can ask for help at places such as forums or Facebook groups for podcasters, but I understand if you want to keep your idea under wraps for now and test it on a small circle of friends. Depending on your budget, I will try to suggest a few options.

Just like with everything, this is a small list of sites that I have used. There are unlimited resources on the internet, so don't be restricted by my selection.

***Fiverr*[113]**

Fiverr is one of the most popular freelancing platforms out there, but instead of posting a job, you look through freelancer's profiles and choose the one that suits you the most. The services start at $5 and cost more if you wish to ask for more. I hired a few voice actors from Fiverr to help us with a re-enactment for *Case 12: Katherine Knight*. Most of them were decent, some amazing and some not so great. I don't have to tell you that for $5 you will not get top-quality work, but it doesn't mean that it will be unusable.

Fiverr is hit or miss, but they have an easy service and a transparent rating system that you can use. The vast selection of categories means that you can find help for almost anything that you want. If you have a tiny budget for your logo, start there, and at least you will have something to show.

***Upwork*[114]**

Upwork is a site that I used for a little bit when I was transitioning from my last job to freelance. The platform gets a bad rep from some people, but I would recommend it to anyone who wants to learn some skills, earn money on the side and try it out 'on their own'. I don't want to get into a debate over outsourcing and race to the bottom on pricing. Upwork is what you make of it, but it's a good place to look for a graphic artist, both if you have a small budget or a bit more money to spend.

You can either browse freelancers and their profiles or post a job with description and budget; you will then get proposals from people all around the globe. Select the ones that match your task, invite them for a chat and hire the best one. It's an easy process, and Upwork has an excellent support team if something goes wrong.

Reddit[115]

I can describe Reddit as a large online forum with countless places called 'subreddits' on pretty much anything that you like. Subreddits are gatherings where you can meet like-minded people and talk about hobbies and interests.

There are subreddits for podcasters where you can ask for help with the design and podcast-related issues. You can visit a subreddit for graphic designers and look for help there too; I saw some people asking for podcast design help and getting the answers straight away.

Word of warning is that you don't get any protection or support like with other platforms. It is strictly a one-to-one hire where you need to trust a person to deliver the work.

These are services I tested, but I don't want to leave you with a limited choice, therefore, here are some other sites where you can try your luck.

Freelancer[116]

Similar to Upwork, you can either look through freelancer's profiles or post a job. They are Upwork's biggest competitor, and the platform works in an almost identical way.

People Per Hour[117]

Another freelancing platform, similar to Upwork and Fiverr. You can post a job and look through bids or select a freelancer whose services match your task. People Per Hour is the UK's main site.

99designs[118]

A platform dedicated to design work. It works a bit differently to the other sites. You create a task—for example, a logo for your podcast—and start receiving ideas from designers. You can then look through submitted work and select the one that you like the most. The designer is then chosen as a 'winner' of the contest and earns your money. 99designs sell pricing packages that start with 'Bronze' at $299.

Behance[119]
Behance is a portfolio website for designers, and there you can find professional help. You won't be able to find someone for $5 but if you have a bit more money to spare, go to Behance and look through people's work. By all means, you can post a job there too, but budgets start at $399.

You can message artists that you like and negotiate the rate on your own. It's a good site to find work if you have a bigger task on your hands.

A WORD ON OUTSOURCING

As the world is getting connected, outsourcing will get larger and more prominent in all economies. Don't dismiss outsourcing or think it's only about hiring cheap workers overseas. Outsourcing can mean cheaper labour as much as the possibility of hiring the best talent on the other side of the globe. *Casefile* is the best example of a remote team working with outsourcing.

The Host quickly realised that he couldn't do the show alone and he looked for the best help he could find. Not the cheapest, but the best. At the moment of writing this book, *Casefile*'s team includes the Host, who is Australian, me—a Polish bloke who lives in the UK— Andrew, who is a composer from Seattle, and a team of writers from Australia.

Don't get discouraged and try looking for help beyond a small circle of friends and family, because the person who shares the same passion as you may live half the world away.

ITUNES ARTWORK

As I mentioned before, to submit a podcast to iTunes, you will need an RSS feed as well as a name and artwork. Remember that iTunes has strict specifications[120] when it comes to graphical assets, and if you don't adhere to them, your podcast will get rejected. Let's have a look at the details.

Cover art
First thing's first, you will need cover art (a logo) for your podcast. The cover art is a square image that needs to look good both on the TV screen as well

as on a mobile phone. The exact specifications from Apple are a minimum size of 1,400 × 1,400 pixels to a maximum size of 3,000 × 3,000 pixels. In addition, iTunes recommends JPG files, although PNG are also allowed; I would go with JPG to make sure the logo gets approved.

Once you have cover art, make sure it looks good not only at maximum size but on different sizes such as 600 × 600, 100 × 100, 60 × 60 and even as small as 30 × 30 pixels.

The artwork should be designed in RGB (Red, Green, Blue) colour space, for screen viewing. On the other hand, you have CMYK (Cyan, Magenta, Yellow, Black) used for ink printing, so don't use that space for your design.

The logo must be clear with the name of the podcast and easy to read. Different podcasting apps may cover different parts of the graphic. Usually, adverts will mask the bottom of the artwork so plan for this kind of details.

When you look at the *Casefile* logo, you can see the perfect example of a straight to the point message. It's a minimalistic design with the clear name of the show, which is visible even when the image is scaled down to 30 × 30 pixels size. It's worth also noting that iTunes also recommends compressing the files.

Apart from that, other requirements, such as the usage of profanity or sexual graphics, apply too. It is the same as with the content of your show.

iTunes feature and über

Let's now talk about other artwork for iTunes that many people might not know about, and the first one is iTunes feature.

When you go to iTunes store on a computer, at the top of the app, you will have a few selected and advertised podcasts. That section of the app is called 'the feature'. iTunes runs campaigns throughout the year, and they decide which podcasts are 'worthy' of being up there, advertised to millions. I don't need to mention that it can make your subscription numbers shoot through the roof. When *Casefile* was featured on iTunes last year, for a brief period, we were number 4 on Top Charts.

To get featured on the iTunes homepage you will need to be contacted by someone from iTunes store (which won't happen) or contact them yourself. Unfortunately, without the leverage a growing audience for your show you probably won't be included in their campaigns, but once your podcast is gaining momentum, look for people responsible for iTunes content management and start hustling.

If you are hosting with a reputable podcasting provider, ask them if they have any connections. More than likely they will. I don't have to mention that the artwork must be top quality and attractive to potential listeners. You will have one shot at that, so no pressure!

Another graphic that you may encounter on the iTunes store is über, from the German word for 'over'. It is the background 'skin' or art that some podcasts have. To see what I'm talking about, go to the iTunes store, on your computer, and look for the *Casefile* or *Lore*[121] podcast, and go to the show's main page. As you can see, instead of a default white background, both shows have a graphic 'skin' that makes the whole page look exceptional. Again, this is only possible on custom request.

You will need to hustle to get it done, either by yourself or with the help of people who are helping you with the show. There are thousands of shows submitted to iTunes each week. They won't respond to everyone and, just like with everything, they will help the 'unicorns'.

Don't despair and work hard on the show. Once you gain popularity, only then start to worry about these aspects of your podcast. We changed our website, logo and art after six months of steady growth and weekly episode releases. At that point, we were already up to hundreds of thousands of listens per month.

Here are the specifications for the über: 4,320 × 1,080 pixels with a resolution of 72 ppi with three cropped areas.

GOOGLE PLAY MUSIC ARTWORK

If you want to have your podcasts available on Google Play, you will also need an artwork that adheres to their specifications.[122] The requirements are similar to iTunes, with a minimum of 600 × 600 pixels and maximum of 7,000 × 7,000. To be featured on Google Play, the artwork must be a minimum size of 1,200 × 1,200; therefore, the same graphic you uploaded to iTunes can be used.

> **NOVEMBER 2019 UPDATE**
>
> Google has now released their podcasting app – Google Podcasts. It transferred the show automatically as it grabs the info and artwork from our hosting service.

SOCIAL MEDIA ARTWORK

Social media has become a part of life, especially in a globalised and computerised world. Social media allows for direct contact with your listeners; I will talk about the strategies for social platforms in the next chapter. For now, let's focus on the visual aspect of it.

Facebook

There are plenty of online guides on the perfect cover for your Facebook page. Once you have the primary logo, you will also need to think about the cover art. The good thing is that once you have the graphic, you can also use it as your iTunes feature or background skin.

Facebook displays two versions of a cover, one on a desktop with specifications 828 × 315 pixels on computers and the other at 640 × 360 pixels for mobiles. The important thing is to test how your cover will look with different sizes, especially desktop vs. mobile.

Instagram/YouTube/Twitter

Instagram
Profile Photo size: 110 × 110 px minimum.

YouTube
Cover Art:
Minimum dimension for upload: 2,048 × 1,152 px.
Minimum safe area for text and logos: 1,546 × 423 px.
Maximum width: 2,560 × 423 px.

File size: 4MB or smaller.
YouTube profile picture size: 800 × 800 px.

Twitter
Header size: 1,500 × 500 px.
Profile size: 400 × 400 px.

You can find the artwork requirement on each platform's support page, but the principle is the same. Always compare desktop vs. mobile, and how your fans view the page. Podcasts are all about the audio, but when people come to your social pages, they look at your posts and graphics, so don't forget the importance of that aspect.

We run a Facebook page, which is our main point of contact, as well as Twitter, and this year we've also started an Instagram account and Patreon.[123] For all of these, we used the same logo and cover artwork – consistency is the key to everything.

EPISODE ART AND TEMPLATES

Having an artwork for each episode is a nice touch. You can feature it on your website as well as a thumbnail for the metadata on the audio file. Depending on the structure of your blog, the size of the episode artwork will change; again, just make sure it looks both good on computers and mobile phones. For the metadata thumbnail the only requirement is that it needs to be square to look good.

I hope I don't need to add that templating your graphics is the key. Go to the *Casefile* website and have a look at the artwork for all the episodes. The image is the same, just the number of the episode and the name changes. Once the template was created, it takes two minutes to adjust it for the latest episode.

We have two templates, one for square, thumbnail art and another for a widescreen image. The hard part is to create the first one, after that, you can just work with the templates.

Make sure that the episode's name is easy to read and it's a good idea to feature the number of the episode too. Also, check if it's easily visible on smartphones.

---

113 Fiverr (*https://www.fiverr.com*)
114 Upwork (*https://www.upwork.com*)
115 Reddit (*https://www.reddit.com*)
116 Freelancer (*https://www.freelancer.com*)
117 People Per Hour (*https://www.peopleperhour.com*)
118 99designs (*https://99designs.co.uk*)
119 Behance (*https://www.behance.net*)
120 iTunes Resources and Help (*n 41*)
121 Lore podcast (*http://www.lorepodcast.com*)
122 Google Play Music (*https://play.google.com*)
123 Patreon (http://patreon.com)

SOCIAL MEDIA, WEBSITE AND NEWSLETTER

It's safe to say that social media is now part of everyday life. Social media provides ways of communication, engagement and receiving direct feedback. For the first time in history, we can contact our 'heroes', ask them questions and receive a reply in an instant. We get to have a look 'behind the scenes' of everything and documenting the journey became as important as the final result. It also allows for scalability; it doesn't matter if you are living at the end of the world, you could send me a tweet or post a comment, and you can be sure that I will at some point read it.

Podcasts are a perfect example of a medium that is scalable, and podcasting is on the rise. As everything goes mobile, more people tune into their favourite hosts, stories and content. Thanks to mobile phones, it's easy to start with a click of a button.

You can run a podcast without a website or social media account; I'm not saying that it is not possible. But, if you want to reach more people and change your listeners into fans, then I would recommend starting on social media straight away.

Casefile was a bit weird when it comes to the social side. For the first few months when we were doing the podcast we didn't track the numbers that much, nor did we pay any attention to social. Our Facebook[124] and Twitter[125] were only for posting new episodes; we hadn't been engaging much there either. Once we realised that we might have something special, I offered help, and together with the Host we started running the social media side the way we should have from the beginning.

Not all was lost – as I'm typing this sentence, we have over 10k likes on Facebook with around 600 new visitors every week, over 6k followers on

Twitter and over 2k on Instagram, all organic traffic. Our posts get high engagement, and we try to post content every day, even if it's a photo or a small update.

I wanted to write this chapter with advice and a few tips. However, I realise that your situation may be, and will be, unique. There are many social platforms that you can focus your time on, platforms that we are not using, such as Snapchat,[126] Musical.ly,[127] YouTube. Even though we are not posting there, the same principles apply—post original content and 'feel the room'. Research why people are using a platform, what kind of content they are looking for and how you can add value to the environment.

NOVEMBER 2019 UPDATE

Our social media presence is growing to this day and the biggest changes were to our Facebook group – one official and one unofficial as well, as a Reddit channel run by the fans. We've also started publishing episodes on YouTube using Repurpose[128] software.

PLATFORMS

Facebook, Instagram, Snapchat, Twitter, Google+, YouTube, Tumblr, Pinterest, LinkedIn, MySpace (is it still a thing?): drop everything you are doing and start signing up for new accounts! Just kidding, but as you can see there are many different social platforms, and they come and go all the time.

There is little point in me giving advice on how to run social media, given the fact that there are much better people out there writing courses and books about that. My advice, taken from my experience, is not to spread yourself too thin. Internet celebrity in one space may impress you, and then the next day you will discover someone new you want to follow, it's normal, and it's called a 'shiny object syndrome'. Instead of focusing on one thing, we often jump on the 'hype train' for new, exciting features and options.

Speaking of possibilities, thanks to the internet, these are now endless.

When you decide to start a podcast, it will probably begin with just you, or maybe as many as two people. Between writing, recording and editing episodes, there won't be a lot of time left in a day to create and run multiple social accounts, I can guarantee that. Focus on one or two that are the closest to the theme of the podcast and start small. Develop an audience, and if you gain in popularity, you can slowly expand your project.

Like I said, with *Casefile* we didn't run social media for the first six months. Only when we realised that people were sharing our content and following us on social media did we start paying more attention to it. We only had Facebook and Twitter to start with, and in the second half of 2016 I started helping out with running both accounts, creating micro-content and updating our listeners with current affairs.

We didn't have Instagram until the beginning of 2017, and we have just launched an email newsletter. It wasn't planned or strategized in the beginning, and we learnt as we went along. Find out what you are good at and what makes sense for your show. Snapchat may be 'hot' right now, but it wouldn't make much sense for *Casefile*. The Host is anonymous, and the only person to run it could be me, and I doubt that many individuals would like to watch me edit audio for hours.

I think it's safe to say that Facebook is the most neutral option out there right now. Almost everyone is on Facebook, and it's easy to direct your listeners there, having a page would be a good move.

The rest are debatable, Twitter is alright, but it's recently been losing popularity (although, apparently it's back now!). Instagram is huge, and we are slowly starting to post content there, but we are already stretched thin with the production of the show, so we'll see how it goes. Big businesses have social media managers to run operations for them; we are not a big business or anything of that kind, but maybe in the future we could hire help.

That's another thing, ask around your friends and family members for help. Maybe you have someone who wants to start a social media agency and can help you out for free to gain experience and to learn the craft. Start frugal, improvise but be mindful of your time. Producing a fantastic podcast should be a priority; you don't want to skimp on the quality of your episodes just because you were making social media posts all day.

ENGAGEMENT

I can describe social media with one word: community. Your social media strategy can and should include marketing; however, your priority should be building a community and establishing an audience that will listen and await your podcast. Your job is to turn your listeners into fans.

To understand why this is so important, I urge you to Google *1,000 True Fans*[129] by Kevin Kelly, where he lays out a blueprint on how you can build a business around your passion project. In short, if you can find a 1,000 people who are willing to spend $100 each on your products, be it a podcast, music, whatever, then you will have a 'salary' of 100k per year, doing what you love. Easier said than done, but if you follow that principle, you will get why it is crucial to build a small community around your show.

At *Casefile* we are proud of the fact that we read every comment, every email or message from the fans. We encourage submitting ideas for episodes and, before making a big decision, we always try to check with our listeners. Hence authenticity and sincerity should play a central role in any business you choose to start. Especially with an entertainment format, such as podcasts, the listener decides to spend time with your show. I find it both humbling and fascinating. Trying to comprehend that there are thousands of people who decide to spend their time listening to our production keeps us grounded and pushes us to do our best. More so when you think that changing stations or deleting them is as easy as a push of the button.

Don't think of your listeners as potential customers; try to build long-lasting relationships instead. We are all fans of something, and we all get stoked when an idol replies to our comment, even likes it. It means that he or she read it. It doesn't take too long to reply—at the moment, both I and the Host reply on social media as well as to Patreon posts. Whenever I have a spare minute, I check any notifications to see if someone posted a question or a comment.

The only thing is the time difference, as many of our listeners are in the USA. This means that, after I wake up, I can see the comments and posts from their evening, but it has still worked rather well so far, despite the delay.

Another thing is likes and followers. As almost all of us seek external validation, there is no better boost to our ego than a lot of new likes or followers. I'll get to it in the next chapter, but I'm against the buying of followers with ads promoting the page. All of our likes and traffic come organically, meaning that people manually look for our page and click the like button. It means that they do want to explore additional content and are interested in what we have to say, keeping the engagement rate high. And that's what counts the most: engaged fans that like your content and are hungry for more.

NOVEMBER 2019 UPDATE

Essentially, we are still in charge of the social media channels, however, we also now have a help from moderators who monitor and organise the groups on Facebook.

WEBSITE AND NEWSLETTER

I am of the belief that everyone should have at least a simple internet site, especially if you want to start a venture such as a podcast. Most of the downloads will happen via mobile phones, but some people still listen to podcasts on their computers. My friend is one of them; she is a photo retoucher, and she listens to *Casefile* while working, streaming it from our website.

I wouldn't push for an expensive site at the start. There are many solutions, such as Wix[130] or Squarespace,[131] that are both cheap and easy to use. At a level above that, you can buy a theme and customise it; the guys from Elegant Themes[132] are one of the best out there. Don't stress too much about it in the beginning. A simple blog where you can upload latest episodes will do. Our current website is far from perfect, and we have plans to change it in the future, but at the moment it is not a priority.

The first one was just a simple WordPress[133] blog, but once we realised that we were getting a few thousand visits a month, we quickly upgraded the site to make it a little bit more appealing. At the moment we have around 150k visits per month, and the site needs an update, but that will come with time. I'd recommend you follow the same tactic, don't rush into unnecessary distractions and don't spend money when you are just starting out.

Another thing to consider when you start a website is running a blog alongside your podcast as it can help to grow your audience and bring additional traffic. However, list your priorities and focus on things that matter. We pondered blogging for a few months, and we even had a few offers from people who wanted to write for us. For now, we declined as it would take away time and focus from the thing that we need to work on—the podcast. Start small and, as your show grows, develop your infrastructure and tools.

Another thing altogether is an email newsletter. We began one in January 2017, and it is one thing that I regret we didn't start earlier. Not enough hours in a day, though.

An email newsletter is an excellent tool for marketing as well as bringing extra content to your fans. People subscribe to your list and, whenever you wish, you could send a 'newsletter', an email with updates, promotions, content and other things related to your show. You know that, by subscribing, your fans allow you to send out these emails, as long as they are not spam or too frequent. I'd recommend at least learning a bit about email marketing and building email campaigns. You don't need to start straight away but also don't wait a whole year before starting one, especially if your show is gaining popularity. The service we use is called MailChimp,[134] and it's free to use for up to 2,000 subscribers.

Of course, there are many other providers, such as Convertkit[135] or Aweber,[136] just to name a couple. However, I haven't used them, so you need to do your research. Start with a free one. Most of the email marketing solution providers offer a free version of their product so take advantage of it to learn the strategies. The newsletter will also help with getting sponsors. We give a shout-out to our sponsors at the bottom of each newsletter, and it's a perk that we offer to businesses that want to advertise on the show. We don't charge anything for it; we provide it as something extra.

124 Facebook (*n 2*)
125 Twitter (*n 39*)
126 Snapchat (*https://www.snapchat.com*)
127 Musical.ly (*https://musical.ly/en-US*)
128 Repurpose (*https://repurpose.io*)
129 Kevin Kelly – 1000 True Fans (*http://kk.org/thetechnium/1000-true-fans*)
130 Wix (*https://www.wix.com*)
131 Squarespace (*https://www.squarespace.com*)
132 Elegant Themes (*https://www.elegantthemes.com*)
133 WordPress (*https://wordpress.com*)
134 MailChimp (*https://mailchimp.com*)
135 Convertkit (*https://convertkit.com*)
136 Aweber (*https://www.aweber.com*)

MARKETING

Marketing and sales are the bedrock of every business. Without marketing, there are no sales, and without sales... well, there is no business. I know that podcasting is not a 'business' in the strictest definition of the word, but I want you to start thinking about it in that way. Not in regards to making money and profit, but getting listeners to tune into your show. Any successful content creator will tell you that the secret lies in 50% creative work and 50% marketing, that is how this world works.

Can you remember how many times you have seen something you liked but it left you wondering why it wasn't more popular? And why other products, which sometimes seem mediocre, are more successful? The answer lies in the marketing.

More than often, successful products have teams of people working on marketing campaigns behind the scenes and have a lot of money to spend on the advertisement. My guess is that you have neither. Don't worry, *Casefile* was also started without any marketing whatsoever and look where we are now. The internet changed how things work, advertisement and 'sponsored posts' still bombard us every day, but it's possible to get recognition and worldwide popularity without spending any money.

I was sceptical too. I studied Music Business for a little while and, listening to the 'top dogs' of the industry, I was shocked when I learnt how every band, every song, every 'discovery' was always pre-planned and paid for with marketing dollars. My naïve worldview was shattered.

It wasn't until *Casefile* that I realised that it was possible to get recognition without marketing. It's rare, but possible. And just because it is hard, does it mean that you should stop trying? Most things that are worth having are hard to come by. Otherwise, everyone would be doing it. Now, I don't want you to think that it is enough to create a podcast, upload it online and wait. Unless you strike it lucky, you will have to do a bit of work too; we still do it every day. Even if you get a taste of 'virality' with your content, at some point you will hit a plateau—a point where you won't grow anymore and will need to do some work.

After a year working on *Casefile* I can say that, to get to that level, you need both virality and marketing. I know, much easier said than done. I don't assume that, after *Casefile*, I could start another podcast tomorrow and get the same results. That's not how it works. But, I began to understand how and why it worked the way it did and what kind of elements you need to repeat the process.

In this chapter, I want to give you a few practical tips on marketing and spreading the word about your podcast, things that everyone can do on a minimal to non-existent budget.

What about getting your podcast going 'viral'? There are a few elements that, in my opinion, help your content to spread. The first one is luck, and you can't cheat it. Why is a particular video or meme shared more than others? It's a snowball effect. It doesn't mean that you have to stop trying, the more chances you take the bigger the possibility of getting 'lucky', but I think we should recognise that hard work, albeit important, is not always enough.

Next, is riding the 'trend' wave. Have a product that people want, not that you want. With *Casefile* it is easy to explain. The rise of shows like *Serial*[137] or *Making a Murderer*,[138] among hundreds of others, showed that the genre, although always popular, was gaining traction. Therefore, shows like *Casefile* had a higher chance to gain popularity.

Where is the luck part? Well, you can't always force getting on the latest trend. An example would be me starting a true crime podcast, just because I know that these kinds of shows are popular. Although I was always fascinated by the crime genre, with writers such as Agatha Christie[139] being some of my favourites, it would be hard for me to do the kind of research the Host of *Casefile* does. I just don't have that much passion for it.

So, as you can see, it takes a bit of luck that what you like to do is also the same thing that a lot of people want to listen to, watch or read. To give an example, as of January 2017, political podcasts are gaining in popularity.

That is to do with recent developments in the USA. The question is, should you start one now? Do you have enough passion for running it for more than a year? And what happens when people look for the next 'hot' thing, will you continue your show? These are the questions you should be asking yourself.

Another thing I noticed about 'virality' is stories. People like to tell and listen to stories, and share them. It's been the case for thousands of years now; it's part of human existence, from drawing on cave walls to internet shows. When I examine *Casefile*, I can say that the way it is structured is based on telling a story. You don't know what is going to happen. You can make your assumption as you listen to the episode and you feel like you are a part of it. The fact that the stories are true adds another layer to the whole premise. It makes it exciting, scary and addictive.

When you are thinking about your show, think how you can tell a story, even if it's a podcast about sports or business. Tell a story, give people a context and something to connect with, and then you will have a bigger chance to stand out.

Another element is uniqueness. How is *Casefile* unique from other true crime podcasts? I wouldn't know, because I don't listen to the other podcasts, and the same goes for the Host. The uniqueness of the show is that we never compared it to anything; we have just been doing our thing. His way of being different was to tell unbiased true crime stories, keep it mysterious to the end and make the research the centre of the show. The details, the depth, the dedication. My thing was that I never worked on that kind of project before, therefore I wasn't limited by any rules. My experience with working on movies meant that I treated the podcast as I would do film production. It means attention to details, top-notch quality, scoring and creative editing. All the tools that I learnt at the film studio I passed on to that project, not only technical but also creative. I believe that it made the whole venture unique and it still does.

Don't necessarily compare yourself to others. By doing that you will learn the rules, and sometimes ignorance is bliss. Especially when you are talking about entertainment and marketing. Of course, let's not forget about the accent of the Host. The fact that he is Australian also played a significant factor, although he always denies it!

Think what makes you different from the others and make it the centre of your project, be proud of it and don't conform to the rules. Otherwise, you will be lost in a sea of mediocrity.

The quality of the product is the last element on my list. If your production is subpar, don't be surprised that people are not sharing it. The first few episodes of *Casefile* weren't that great either. The Host realised that he had something special and needed help with production. Once I jumped on board, with every episode we started to improve, and when we realised that the show was growing, we made another jump in production, at around episode twenty-something.

It takes a lot of work to get to that level—experience, professional tools and time also play a role. When you have thousands of ears listening to your show, it adds the pressure too. So, if you are planning on going 'viral' consider that it will take a lot of time and effort; there is no such thing as an 'overnight' success. We think that just because we don't see how much preparation and work it took to release that video, song or podcast. I'm not only talking about actual work, but also about years of experience under your belt, experience that you put to use. I always say that it takes the right place, the right time and the right set of skills to have all the stars aligned.

Let's now jump to the second part of the chapter, actionable tips on marketing the first podcast.

Family & friends

That one is obvious. Start with people you know and ask them to share your podcast. Invite them to like you Facebook[140] page, ask if they can invite their friends. It all starts small, and don't neglect your close ones. Your friends may have someone who will like the show and pass it forward to another person, who in turn will like it, and so on and on.

It looks better, even if it's just for your ego, to have these few listens and likes. I'm not saying you should rely on your friends and family; they will listen to your show because you asked them to and probably won't offer you unbiased feedback. However, it's a safe place to start.

Word of mouth
That's the best kind of marketing and the hardest to control. It's linked to family and friends. Ask yourself; will you rather take a recommendation from your friend or a stranger? That's why the power of word of mouth is so amazing and can make or break your show. I don't really need to add that you are looking for positive word of mouth.

Here is a bit of advice on how you can 'help' to spread the word. Add 'like and share' on your Facebook posts; add 'please RT' (re-tweet) on your Twitter[141] updates; study both relevant and popular hashtags on Instagram[142] and use them to gain followers. With time you can also include a short CTA (call-to-action) at the beginning and the end of the podcast.

Ask your listeners to follow you on social media, to review the show and pass it forward. Make the content both accessible and attractive to share. Ask yourself, if you were the listener, would you share the post on your feed?

Groups, forums, Reddit
Another way to market your podcast is to be active in places where people care about the kind of content you are creating. Let's say you want to start a podcast about board games. The likely scenario is that you like to play board games and talk about them. The advice would be to find Facebook groups for board gamers and look for sites like Board Game Geek,[143] or relevant subreddits, and start participating. Don't push your podcast but have a link to it somewhere in a description of your profile. Talk to others, build relationships and, when there is a time and a place, mention the podcast. Remember, no one likes spam.

The same tip goes for anything you want to do—fitness, true crime, politics, comedy shows. Find a group of like-minded people and share your stories with them. Besides, take part in groups or forums dedicated to podcasters in general, there are plenty of them around. Even at Reddit,[144] you have one sub /r/podcasts and another called /r/audio drama, where you can post all things podcast related. Just make sure you are doing it in a tactful and respectful way.

Blogs

You have two options and can do both at once. One is to have a blog on your site with optimised posts that will bring you traffic from the search engines. It's a good idea, but it's also a lot of work. Unless you have a helping hand, it will take time away from creating a podcast. At *Casefile* we often talk about starting a blog or paying someone to do it for us, but at the moment we have neither time nor funds to pursue the idea, but it's on a future agenda.

The second option is other people's blogs and press. With *Casefile*, we were lucky enough that a few blogs featured us on their podcast recommendation lists; we also got a shout-out on a few YouTube channels. It helps to grow the audience and gain new listeners.

Remember when I said about the recommendations from a trusted source? It works in the same way. Now, it will be hard for you to get a mention on a big blog or a site, especially in the beginning. Once you gain some traction and leverage, you can start making those relationships. Let me give you an example of the process.

I may search for 'best true crime podcasts list' on Google and see what comes up. More than likely, I will find a few blog posts on the subject. If you see something that was popular but hasn't listed *Casefile*, I may try to contact the author of the post. What would I say? Well, probably something along the lines of – I read the post and enjoyed it, and that if they are planning on updating the list, I would recommend checking out *Casefile*. That the posts will then be shared on our social media accounts with XX followers and posted on our website with XX monthly visits.

As you can see, it's a win-win for both parties. We would get exposure to their audience, and they would get new readers from our sites—look for opportunities like that.

In the beginning, you may target small blogs and sites, someone who just started out and is looking for content. Maybe they will have a 'new, excellent podcasts' list or something of that kind. There is always the possibility that they will check out yours and feature it. If you don't ask you will never get. With time it's the same, like with everything else, the bigger you get, more people will talk about you without even asking. But when you are starting out, you need to work for it.

Podcasting networks

Another way to speed up the growth is to join a podcasting network. I'm not going to recommend one. There are plenty of them around, just Google '(your podcast subject) podcasting network'. Sports, fitness, business, true crime, comedy, there is a place for all. But, what are podcasting networks?

They are collections of podcasts under one umbrella, a publisher who helps with acquiring sponsors as well as the cross-promotion of the show. There will more than likely be a fee and it will be a % of your sponsorship money, anything between 20–50 per cent, with 30% being a standard.

Podcasting networks are helpful when you want to focus on making a podcast and need help with everything else, podcast business related. People who run these networks have knowledge and connections in the podcasting world and will help you get to the next level. Check out what is available in your genre and contact people who run the networks. Listen to the podcasts that they feature and, if you think you are a good match, let them know that.

When you are getting big on your own, these networks will contact you directly, and the offers will keep coming. However, if you are starting out, you are one of many and will have to make the first move. So don't wait for anybody else and start hustling!

Other podcasts

Cross-promotion is another way to gain new listeners. Pair up with other podcasts of the same genre and give a shout-out to each other on the shows. Podcasting is not a zero-sum, every podcast is different and you can win by offering help. The method would be to cross-promote on similar shows, so you both find people who will enjoy the content, but remember to target similar levels of popularity.

If you are starting out you won't be able to do that with someone that gets a million downloads. There is nothing that you can offer to that person, and it becomes a one-way street. Always look for win-win scenarios. Better yet, try to give more value to the other person, this way you won't sound desperate which, especially in negotiation, gives you an upper hand.

With time, you will be offered paid cross-promotion as other podcasters will want to 'tap' into your audience and advertise. It's up to you if you feel that listeners will enjoy the other show, and if you are happy with the money.

Create a list of similar shows that you can add value to and ask the authors if they want to do a free cross-promotion. You can offer social shout outs, call to actions on your episode, mentions on the site and newsletter and other things related. Look for win-win scenarios, and you will never lose.

Charts, reviews, subscriptions

I don't need to say that being a feature on top charts, iTunes home page or having an episode on the "most popular" list helps. It's like with everything else; it's easy to make money once you have it, it's easy to gain new clients once you have plenty of experience and referrals. But how can you get to that position?

I don't need to say that being a feature on top charts, the iTunes home page or having an episode on the 'most popular' list helps. It's like with everything else; it's easy to make money once you have it, it's easy to gain new clients once you have plenty of experience and referrals. But how can you get to that position?

iTunes won't feature you on the top of their store unless you are a 'big' show already. But you can make it to New & Noteworthy, and that will boost your downloads. Focus on reviews and subscriptions. You need to direct listeners to help you to grow the show. Reviews will help with social proof and the more reviews you have, the better. But, it won't assist you with getting on the charts; here is where subscriptions come in.

The algorithm works on how many subscriptions your podcast gets in a period. Why? It's easy to game reviews, to pay for the reviews and to gather fake ones. It's not so easy to pay for subscriptions, as the listeners need to have Apple ID accounts. The more subscriptions you get in a short time, the higher you will climb. The perfect example would be *Casefile* last year.

When we got a feature on the iTunes home page, for a brief period, we climbed to number four on the top charts. At the moment, we are hovering around the top fifty, sometimes we fall to the seventies and sometimes we go up to thirties. Downloads and reviews don't matter as much for the top charts' algorithm. When we featured on iTunes homepage, a lot of people subscribed to the show, in a period of a week or so. That gave us the boost for the charts that resulted in even more people subscribing.

The moral of the story is not to neglect these principles. Make sure to ask listeners to subscribe and review your show. Get noticed and get on the charts!

Ads and Influencers

Here comes the controversial topic: paid traffic. Should you do it? There are pros and cons to everything, but first of all, let me be clear: at *Casefile* we never paid for traffic nor had a sponsored post. All the likes and follows we have come from the fans and listeners, actual human beings.

With ads you have a few options: Facebook and Instagram ads, Google AdWords,[145] boosting your posts and influencer marketing. Facebook and Instagram ads are paid sponsored posts. You can advertise your whole page or single posts. Boosting a post on Facebook is making sure that more of your fans will see your content. Google AdWords are banner ads that you get when browsing the internet. Influencer marketing is paying someone with a following to give you a shout-out on his or her social channels.

These are the main options you have, so let me give you my two cents on each of them, and remember that I'm talking about promoting a podcast, not selling a product. Facebook and Instagram ads are a no for me. There is some proof that if you are just promoting a page, then a lot of the likes will be 'fake'. To check a video that explains it in detail look up 'veritasium Facebook fraud'[146] on YouTube. He explains what clicking farms are and why promoting a page for money is sort of similar to buying fake likes.

As I mentioned before, it's all about engagement. As for now all the likes and follows on our social accounts are organic, meaning that real people manually search for *Casefile* and click the like button. Hence why our posts get a lot of likes and comments. What would you prefer—100,000 likes with no engagement or 1,000 fans who like, share and comment on every post?

Bear that in mind when you are thinking of running an ad for a page. Many people will click the like button but never visit your page or podcast, and the whole point is to get more listeners.

Google AdWords is similar. I haven't tested them for a podcast, but think about the ROI (return on investment). Each click will cost money, and with podcasts, you are not selling anything. The cost to get a few thousands of listeners could be huge, and I would stay with free methods of marketing your show.

Boosting your post on Facebook is a bit different. We haven't tried it with *Casefile* yet, but we will in the future once we have a bit more funds for marketing. What is it exactly? Let's say you have 10k likes on Facebook. When you make a new post, only a small percentage will see it on their feeds. It depends on various factors, but you will never get all of your fans to look at it. Boosting a post means paying Facebook for showing your content to more of your fans, people who liked the page. So instead of 20% of them, 50% will see it.

This, I think, has a lot of value, especially if you are posting something that you wish more people saw, a promotion or merchandising campaign.

Influencer marketing is also something that sits on my mind. Only recently we got a shout-out on a popular YouTube channel. It wasn't paid or anything, the author is a fan of the show and shared it with her audience. Thanks to that, we had quite a few people messaging us that they found the podcast through the recommendation. Now imagine paying a lot of these influencers to give your show a shout-out on social channels. Let's say you want to start a podcast about fitness. You could find influencers in the online fitness space and pay them, or offer them something for a CTA on their social accounts. They provide value to their audience by recommending a relevant content and you gain new listeners.

NOVEMBER 2019 UPDATE

As of now, podcast discoverability is still problematic. However, this is slowly changing with platforms like DiscoverPods[147] and Podchaser[148] trying to tackle this issue. On top of that, big companies started to enter podcasting space, which means it is getting more difficult for an independent podcast to market and get exposure without serious campaign and budget.

It's not too late yet. However, if the trend continues in the next few years it will be very, very difficult to break in if you are a beginner podcaster and the process will require signing up with a professional network.

137 Serial (*n 12*)
138 Making a Murderer (*n 9*)
139 Agatha Christie (*http://www.agathachristie.com*)
140 Facebook (*n 2*)
141 Twitter (*n 39*)
142 Instagram (*n 38*)
143 Board Game Geek (*https://boardgamegeek.com*)
144 Reddit (*https://www.reddit.com*)
145 AdWords (*http://www.google.co.uk/adwords/start*)
146 Veritasium Facebook Fraud (*https://www.youtube.com/watch?v=oVfHeWTKjag&t=119*)
147 DiscoverPods (*https://discoverpods.com*)
148 Podchaser (*https://www.podchaser.com*)

PART III

Money

As much as we don't like to admit it, money makes the world go round. It's neither good nor bad, just a statement. Money is a means of exchanging goods and services, and without it, we wouldn't be able to live the way we do. But what about podcasting? Should you get paid for what you do? Is it even a legitimate service?

The same laws apply as with any other business. As long as you offer value to people, you will get something in return. That's just how it works, and money is one of the things that can be offered during the exchange. But, what kind of value does podcasting offer?

Well, it depends on the nature of the podcast. It can be information, entertainment or advice. If you run marketing podcasts, you offer tips about marketing, if you talk about sports, you supply extra info for the fans, or you can do something like *Casefile*, a podcast that offers stories and 'escapism'. It is the same with books, video games or movies. The medium or nature of the content doesn't matter as long as it carries value to the consumer.

There is no shame in making money from podcasting, and you don't need to think about it as 'selling out.' If you have something that is amazing, people will offer their support without asking. It's the same way as supporting anyone else. I regularly make donations to Wikipedia[149] and Khan Academy;[150] these are free services, but over the years I received so much value from these sites I want to help and support them. It's a simple principle of reciprocity: give first, and you can be sure that it will come back to you.

Let's talk about the actual logistics of making money from a podcast. One thing is sure, it will not be easy. Podcasting is not a job or a straightforward business, even though once you get revenue in you should treat it as such. For most parts, you should try to develop multiple sources of income and never rely on one money stream. Podcasting is the 'wild west'. It is still a niche, it is not regulated, and you can experiment as much as you want. Sponsors, products, donations, affiliations, all can work and help to support your show when done right. Don't go into podcasting thinking you will get rich quick. There are plenty of other industries that you should try if your sole goal is to make money—podcasting is not one of them.

It takes a lot of effort, time and resources to produce a great show and any return on that investment is not guaranteed. Even if you have a popular podcast, it may take you a year or two before you start turning a profit, that's average for most businesses anyway. It can be done. It's hard but not impossible, but set your priorities straight. Content first, money later. Engagement with the audience first, revenue later. Community first, swimming in dollars later.

Let's have a look at some ways that you can generate income from a podcast.

---

149 Wikipedia (*https://en.wikipedia.org/wiki/Main_Page*)
150 Khan Academy (*https://www.khanacademy.org*)

SPONSORSHIP

Sponsorship, the Holy Grail for most podcasters. Many podcasters think that when they secure sponsorships, the future of their show will be safe. The money will keep rolling in, and they will sit on the beach sipping cocktails. All the dreams will come true. But, is it really like that? Does sponsorship secure you the income you want? Is it stable enough that you can quit your day job? In this chapter, I want to clarify a few things about sponsors and give you a few tips on how to approach sponsorship in a smart way.

When I started working on *Casefile*, and a few other podcasts, I didn't know much about the medium. I agreed to help out on *Casefile* for a nominal fee as the Host was financing everything from his pocket. The agreement was to re-negotiate once we secured 'sponsorship'.

Back then, *Casefile* was one of many of my side projects. I didn't give it much thought. I carried on with my life. A few months passed and, as the show grew, we started to get offers from advertising networks as well as potential sponsors. "Wow! This is it! We are gonna be rich!" That was the first thought we had. It took us a few moments to realise that it was not as easy as it sounded. I rolled up my sleeves and dived into the depths of the internet.

I started to do what I should have done months before: research how the podcasting world works. As I was reading through blogs and listening to podcasting advice, it all seemed straightforward. Once your podcast gets enough downloads, you get sponsors and get paid. Everyone is happy. But, just like most things that seem too easy, the whole venture turned out to be a bit more problematic than I thought. First thing's first, what is sponsorship and how does it work?

I don't think I need to dwell on a definition of a sponsor. Sponsorship is an advertisement, and it's everywhere. Have a look at the music industry, sports, games, TV, movies, newspapers and everything in between. Advertising is the bedrock of capitalism and one of the pillars of business. Once your content becomes popular, companies will want to get exposure to your audience to get more sales and maximise their own profits. The best advertising campaigns match a product with the public and bring value to people, but it isn't necessary. Marketing done right can sell anything and everything. Why would we associate extreme sports with an energy drink? Or athletic events with sugar water? How you market the product is crucial, otherwise it will hurt your brand and, by extension, your sales. No one in business wants that! So, why are advertisers big on podcasts?

Think about other mediums. YouTube has adverts on popular videos, yet most of us can't wait these five seconds to hit 'skip' button. TV has adverts during the break of your favourite show: for most of us, it is the time to look at the mobile phone and check social media or make a cup of tea. We can omit banner ads with a simple ad-block extension installed within an internet browser. The verdict is clear—most people don't like ads. Why? There is no connection between the advertiser and you. You don't know people behind the brand; you never used their product. Why should you trust them? You view it as a sales pitch, and no one wants to be sold to. We think we can make decisions on our accord; we buy what we want and when we want it. Of course, if that was true it would be a topic for another discussion altogether. If you wish to read more about the subject of choice architecture, I recommend a book called *Nudge*[151] by economist Richard H. Thaler and professor Cass R. Sunstein.

Here is why podcasting shines. Most advertisements featured on the podcasts are built into the episode. The host of the show reads the advert at the beginning of the show, or he/she can incorporate it during the discussion. Similar to product placement in movies, you don't get an advert in the middle of the film, but maybe the mobile phone the hero uses is a famous brand. Product placement is huge business so don't think that, just because it's not an obvious advertisement, it is not there. That's how a lot of YouTubers or Instagram personalities make their living. Companies pay influencers a lot of money so they can wear their clothes, review their products, use their goods.

Sponsors understand the core principle of sales. People are inclined to buy a product recommended by a friend instead of an 'authority'. Even if the 'authority' is the expert in the field. Think about it, let's say you wish to buy a new TV and you not only do your diligent research online, but you also speak to the staff at your local TV store. Everything points towards set A, and then you decided to purchase it. However, a day before, you visit a good friend who is an avid technology geek and just bought a new TV, set B. Not only does he praise the latest buy but also makes a point that B is much better than A. What do you do? Do you follow the research and opinion of the experts or throw it in the bin and go with the recommendation of your friend, whom you know and trust? Most things in life are built on trust, as most things require a relationship with fellow human beings. And what is a better catalyst for sales than trust?

Here comes podcasting, an intimate medium where, after a while of listening to the voice of the host, you feel like you know the person behind it. There is a connection, an established relationship. If you listen to the show because you know it will offer you value with every episode, there is also trust. Advertisers are smart. They understand that if they play a standard radio-style ad during the podcast, most listeners will dismiss it. Hence the hosts read the adverts. Their voice is familiar to thousands, so it doesn't feel like an ad. It feels like a recommendation from a friend, a friend whom you know and have listened to for months.

Hence why it works, and that's why companies are big on podcasters, YouTubers and other social influencers. It's always been that way and always will be. If your sports hero wears a particular pair of boots and recommends it, well, we all want to be like our heroes, right?

Of course, the advertisement can add value if done right, when you recommend the product that you use and believe in. It's important to balance between the two: revenue and adding value to listeners. Both are equally as important in helping to secure the future of your show.

Let's now look at the logistics of podcast advertisement. At the present moment, you have a few analytics available, supported by your hosting company. You can see the country and what percentage of listeners are in each territory, which platform is most popular and the number of downloads; not listens, but downloads. Unfortunately, for now, we can't see more detailed statistics like: when do listeners pause the episode? Do they skip the ads? What is the average lengths of listens? Therefore neither the advertisers, nor you, know how many people listened to their message.

Let's say your hosting service shows that the latest episode was downloaded two million times. How many people listened to it? Were some downloads repeated? Sometimes we download content for later and it sits on the hard drive for months. As you can see, it gets tricky and, unless someone comes up with a tracking method for downloaded podcasts, you won't know for sure how many people have listened to a show.

I guess it's similar to TV; you can never know how many people watched the ad. It's all based on assumptions. The problem with podcasts is that sponsorship is trackable, and TV is not. You will get a unique code that you offer, let's say 'casefile', and only if someone uses it will the sponsors know that the advert on your podcast worked.

It is not a perfect solution, because advertisement often works on a subconscious level; you choose a product because you heard of it, even though you may not remember where you heard about it. A year from now, someone may purchase a product recommended on your podcast, but because they didn't use the special code the advertisers won't know that it was you who brought the customer in, and they may cancel the contract. As I said, it's not ideal.

So you can't guarantee sales as you don't know detailed statistics. What can you offer? Podcast sponsorship is based on CPM measure, cost per mille, that is the cost per thousand impressions. Impressions are your downloads. CPM can range from as little as $10 to as high as $50. However, $20 CPM is somewhat an average rate.

Let's say your podcast is getting 1,000 downloads; you attract a sponsor with $10 CPM rate.

$10 CPM × 1,000 = 10 × 1 = $10 – for that you will get $10.

You can see how it can grow into significant numbers once your show gains in popularity:

$10 CPM × 10,000 = 10 × 10 = $100

$10 CPM × 100,000 = 10 × 100 = $1,000

$10 CPM × 1,000,000 = 10 × 1,000 = $10,000

...and if you double CPM rate to $20 you start seeing how well it can work in your favour. However, I doubt that you will be able to find a sponsor that will pay for one million impressions, especially when you are still establishing the show.

You may get the numbers, but selling them is another story. That's the main point; the sponsors will often have a set number of dollars to spend on the advert. If their marketing budget is $5,000 per ad, it won't matter that you are getting a million or ten million downloads. Once they are happy with the minimum, that's it: the extra impressions will be free.

Of course, if your podcast continues to grow, you get more leverage and can attract bigger companies, but it is not a math game. Do not count each download as a potential dollar. I'll come back with more details about getting paid, for now, so let's focus on what you can sell, what you can offer.

For direct advertising, you can provide 'ad spots' called pre-roll, mid-roll and post-roll. These are similar to standard TV advertisement. You get an ad before the show, during the show and after the show. These vary in CPM, with mid-roll advertisement selling for the highest CPM, then pre-roll and post-roll with the lowest. Sometimes post-roll will be included in an overall budget, so let's say for $3,000 the sponsor will get a pre-roll and post-roll with no extra charge, it depends on the advertiser.

The average length of the ad depends on the read, but it is somewhere between 30–90 seconds for a pre-roll, 30–60 seconds for a mid-roll and a short 30-second ad as a post-roll. Again, it all depends on the deal, marketing budget and contract with each advertiser. It will be up to you how many ad spots you offer. In theory, the more you can sell, the more money you can make. In practice, it doesn't always work like that. I would say that, when it comes to podcast advertising, the law of diminishing returns[152] applies more than ever. One ad is okay, two is passable, three, four, five? At some point listeners won't pay any attention or will be skipping ads, looking for the main content. If sponsors don't see a clear ROI, then they will back out from the deals. It's a question of balance. No one likes ads, except the people who work in advertisement, but listeners tolerate them. Push the tolerance too much, and you will hurt your podcast.

We agreed that having a couple of pre-rolls and post-rolls won't hurt, given the length of the episodes. If we were doing a 15-minute show, then we wouldn't include three to four minutes of advertising. My point being, there is no right answer. Every podcast is different, and you will have to decide what is best for yours. Remember, once you go down the route of sponsorship, prepare for a negative feedback from some listeners. My advice would be to keep the ads balanced and not intrusive, which will help to minimise the criticism from the fans.

Now you know how adverts on podcasts work, the question is: where can you get the sponsors? There are a few ways to do that. First would be to hustle. If your podcast is around a specific topic in a particular industry, you can approach companies and ask them if they would be interested in advertising on the show. Of course, you will need to offer them some value for money, if your show gets a few downloads per episode, no one will sponsor you. I have to admit that we haven't done that. First of all, it would be quite difficult to find someone, given the subject of *Casefile*, and second, we focused on making the show as good as possible. Sponsorship was the last thing on our minds.

That leaves us with the second way to get sponsorship, wait till they approach you. Believe me, once you gain some traction, you will get offers from all over the place, as there are people who are scouting the space for popular podcasts. Just to be clear, you probably won't be approached by companies, but by advertising networks that handle marketing budgets and, if you are big enough, they will offer a sponsorship deal. Deals can be either for one or multiple episodes, and it depends on how established your podcast is.

The third way is to get help, and help comes in the form of podcasting networks; I mentioned them in the last chapter. Podcasting networks will assist you in marketing and growing your podcast, and can help you to secure sponsorship. Let's be honest, if you are starting out or are learning how podcasting works, it will be hard to produce episodes and take care of ad sales. Signing a contract with a podcasting network can take some of that burden away, not for free of course.

For the sales, the networks earn commission from your ads—this will be between 20–50% of every ad sold. Podcasting networks work with advertisement agencies, and they take another 'slice of the pie'.

Let's take a step back and look at the available options:

YOU – COMPANY
Direct ad sales, you make all the dollars.

YOU – AD AGENCY – COMPANY
Ad agency takes a cut. They won't work directly with you unless you are a big name in podcasting.

YOU – PODCASTING NETWORK – AD AGENCY – COMPANY
Network and agency take a cut. This is the most standard model as agencies talk to your representative (networks) and you only have to deal with the networks.

The ideal scenario would be working directly with companies. However, big corporations don't talk to podcasters, and if you are planning on selling 500k impressions and up, only the big companies will be able to afford that kind of sponsorship.

There are other options, such as having an 'agent' that represents you. However, every additional 'team member' will take away some of the revenue. If the pie is big enough, everyone gets to eat, but if you are operating on a smaller level, watch out: otherwise, you will only get the crumbs.

Let's have a look at the three big ones that offer help with advertising.

Blubrry

I mentioned their service in the chapter about hosting. Turns out they also help with setting up advertisements for podcasters.[153] At present they have two programs you can sign up to: one is a casual advertising deal, where you get ads per episode and can back out anytime you want. The revenue share split it 50/50.

Another one is called Priority Partner, and even though it is still not exclusive, you will need to sign a contract and commit to running multi-episode campaigns. It helps to plan for longer than just one or two episodes and develop deeper relationships with sponsors. The revenue share split is 70/30.

Libsyn

Libsyn[154] is another hosting service that offers help with sponsorship. To be able to opt in for advertising services with Libsyn, your show must have more than 20k downloads per month. You get to pick custom ad slots and have the final say on advertisers. The revenue share split is 50/50, but as your show grows and bigger campaigns are available, your share can grow to as high as 70/30.

Midroll

Midroll[155] is a podcasting network and the biggest one out there. They match podcasters with advertisers and own platforms such as Stitcher and Howl.

Once you sign up to their services, you get access to the app that handles all the logistics. You can apply for ad campaigns, review advertisers and control your revenue. The split share is 70/30.

Remember, these are only the three bigger ones. There are many podcasting networks, hosting services that can help you with securing advertisers and growing the show. It's best to do research before you commit to anything and study other successful podcasts. What are they doing? Where are they hosting? What kind of sponsorship do they have? Learn from them, copy their tactics and, once you get to their level, you can start setting up the rules.

What else can you offer advertisers? Some hosting services such as ART19[156] started offering geo-targeting, that is you can select the territory where the ad is played. On one episode, you can have one ad played only to an Australian audience, and the other one played only to American listeners.

There is also an option of ad insertion technology. For example, when we run an ad before a *Casefile* episode, it will stay there forever: it was manually inserted into the audio file with the main content. Another way is to use ad insertion that is 'stitching' a separate audio file with an advert to your episode. Once it reaches the impression goal, you can 'switch off' the ad, and it won't be played again.

Always offer more value than the other party and, with time, it will come back to you in greater numbers. And there is no better leverage than saying at the end of a six week campaign that instead of delivering 300k impressions you produced 2 million—it will make negotiations much easier.

What else can you offer to advertisers? We have a sponsors' page on *Casefile* website. We attract a significant amount of traffic each month, and it is extra exposure for sponsors. It's banner ads for free on a popular site. Apart from that, we run a weekly newsletter, and at the bottom of it, we always put links to the latest episode sponsors; that gives them extra exposure to our audience.

These extras are all a 'cherry on top' and can help you attract advertisers months in advance. Once you know that you have sold campaigns for the next six months, it makes life much easier, and you can focus on what matters the most: producing the best podcast there is.

NOVEMBER 2019 UPDATE

Ads are still the bedrock of the podcasting industry and sponsorship will grow in the coming years as the big companies enter the market.

With the size of the *Casefile* audience we are lucky to be able to negotiate our terms, but the numbers still set how much money from ads you will get. It will be interesting to see how the industry develops in terms of personalised ads, but one thing is for sure, they are here to stay.

GETTING PAID

You secured the sponsorship. Everything is set, you plan to buy new equipment and cover some costs when the money comes in. However, since you ran the ad, days have passed and the money is not in the bank yet. What happened? It's never as easy as it sounds, especially with the sponsors. Hence why I recommend looking for other sources of revenue, which I will discuss in the next chapters.

The ad campaign you secure for an episode is not for one week. The whole campaign is usually 6–8 weeks' worth of impressions. So, if you sold

300k worth of impressions, you have six weeks to deliver on that promise. After six weeks, you review the campaign with the advertisers who, depending on the contract, have additional time to fulfil the invoice. Let's say it's another six weeks, and that's not all. More than likely you will be dealing with a podcasting network that handles the ad money. Depending on the contract, they too take their time to transfer the funds to you—let's assume it is another six weeks.

So you run an ad worth $4,000 in the first week of January. How much and when will you see the money? With 50/50 split you will get $2,000, with 70/30 you will net $2,800.

6 weeks × 3 = 18 weeks
18 weeks × 7 days = 126 days

That's over four months. So, realistically you are looking at the end of the April. If you look at Blubbry Advertising for Podcasters website, they state: 'Payment typically takes eight to twelve weeks after the end of the campaign month. This allows both sides to gather data, confirm final settlement, mail checks and resolve any dispute.'

Eight to twelve weeks after the end of the campaign month. So, if you run a six week campaign at the beginning of January, the end of the campaign month will be February. Add twelve weeks to that, and it totals to five months. End of April, with beginning of May being the worst-case scenario.

As you can see, you will have to wait for the fruits of your labour. Even if you started to secure sponsorship, you would need to work for a few months, producing content without any signs of revenue. So don't go quitting your day job just yet.

NOVEMBER 2019 UPDATE

With growth comes more leverage and you will be able to negotiate earlier payments, but always check the terms and conditions of your network.

CANCELLATIONS

Yes, they do happen, for various reasons. Maybe the marketing budget got slashed, perhaps the company went into administration, and maybe the ad strategy did not work for them. Even if you secure a long-term deal, advertisers have a right to cancel within an agreed period, usually 30 days. You may be happy that a sponsor bought the whole inventory for a month, only to find out that they cancelled at the last moment, and you need to look for someone else. Nothing is set in stone; nothing is permanent. Things can change within a second, with one email. Be ready for it and plan for the worst-case scenario.

What would you do if everyone cancelled the agreement? Do you have enough funds to keep going for a while? Don't wish, strategize and remember that 'failing to plan is planning to fail.'

BANNER ADS AND ADSENSE

Last way to get ad revenue is to display banner ads on your website. You can either negotiate a package with sponsors directly or sign up for Google AdSense[157] as a separate deal. It depends on your traffic and business model. Some businesses such as news publishers make most of their revenue from displaying ads on their sites, so it's an option.

I prefer to offer "Sponsors Page" as the extra value we give to advertisers. Podcasting is not blogging, and you want to drive traffic to the episodes, not the website. Therefore banner ads may not be the best strategy. Apart from that, people hate banner ads more than anything else, and with rising popularity of ad-blocks, it may lead you to a dead end.

But, everyone is different, and it may make perfect sense for you to display banners on the site, maybe for local businesses. Think about it, research the topic, make pros and cons list and try it out. You never know until you try it.

151 Richard H. Thaler, Cass R. Sunstein – Nudge: Improving Decisions About Health, Wealth and Happiness
(*https://www.amazon.com/Nudge-Improving-Decisions-Health-Happiness/dp/014311526X*)
152 Law of Diminishing Returns
(*http://www.economicshelp.org/microessays/costs/diminishing-returns*)
153 Advertising on Blubrry (*https://create.blubrry.com/resources/blubrry-podcast-advertising*)
154 Libsyn (*n 27*)
155 Midroll (*http://www.midroll.com*)
156 ART19 (*https://art19.com*)
157 Google AdSense (*https://www.google.co.uk/adsense/start*)

AFFILIATIONS

Another way to monetise your show is by affiliate marketing. What is it and how can you incorporate it into a podcast? I would describe affiliate marketing as a sales commission. You recommend a product to the potential buyer, and if he or she buys it, you make a percentage of that sale. It's similar to selling insurance or cars, but on the internet you can 'talk' to many people at once, depending on the traffic.

Affiliate marketing is nothing new, and people like Pat Flynn[158] make over a hundred thousand dollars per month with affiliations. You can go to his website and check income reports as he shares his monthly revenue online with his readers. Pat's whole business is based around affiliate marketing, so no wonder he is making a lot of money from it, but you may think it is not the best example. Instead, have a look at a business set up by John Lee Dumas, and yes it's a podcast.

The podcast is called *Entrepreneur on Fire*[159] and, just like Pat Flynn, John Lee Dumas posts his monthly revenue online. He makes around fifty thousand dollars a month from affiliate marketing. I'm not suggesting that this is how much you will be earning when you start a podcast. Both of these guys spent years developing their businesses and are well-known personalities within their niches. They have huge audiences that look for business advice, and they recommend valuable products. Not every podcast will have the same outcome as they did.

Let's say you want to start a comedy show. I'm sure you will find some products you can recommend to your listeners, but it may be much harder to make significant revenue from that. In comparison, if you start a podcast for graphic designers, your pool of options is much bigger. You could recommend courses, software and services with stock graphics. All of these could be a good fit for your show and bring revenue from affiliate marketing. Just like everything, you need to be mindful and aware of your situation. Don't go chasing every opportunity just because someone had success there. If you don't do the research, you may hit a dead end and waste precious time.

We don't do affiliate marketing with *Casefile*, even though we have significant traffic to the website as well as a growing newsletter list. Between working on the show and running the business side of things, it is not a priority right now. On top of that, it could be quite hard to find a good affiliate match for us. Our listeners come to the show to listen to the stories, not for business advice; the model, therefore, is different than EonFire.

Affiliate marketing gets a bad reputation, and it made me a little bit more suspicious on the internet. Once you learn how it works, every 'review' website comes into question. Did they give the product a good review because it is good? Or because of the sales commission? Same with recommendations. Let's say I use tool A for my podcast production, but they don't offer an affiliation option; on the other hand, tool B does. Assume that I have a large audience that listens to my opinion. Do I go with the truth? Or should I go with the one that brings revenue?

These are the questions that you will need to answer if you want to go down that route. As you probably noticed, it's similar to sponsorship or influencer marketing, but you don't get paid for impressions but actual sales. I will assume that you will stay truthful to listeners, and recommend only the products that you use and could be of value to somebody else. What are your options?

Advertising on podcast

The obvious method is to advertise on your podcast. With affiliate marketing you can start straight away, if they accept you into the program. Most product developers will need some kind of proof that you will be a good fit for them. One requirement will be a website; you won't get approved for most programs if you don't host a site for your podcast. To create a CTA (call-to-action) for a product on your podcast you could record it as a typical pre-roll, post-roll or mid-roll ad. Or during your show, you could say the name of the product within the context of your show.

Let's say you run a creative writing podcast; you could recommend Grammarly[160] service to your listeners and offer a discount if they sign up through your link. It doesn't need to be a straight-up advert; the recommendation could be incorporated into the show.

I don't need to mention that once you start growing your download numbers, sponsorship pays more than affiliation, as it's not based on sales. Know when to make the switch.

Advertising on website

This is the most common method for making money with affiliate marketing, and that's how the majority uses the business model. Once you start bringing significant traffic to a website you may want to sign up for affiliate programs. The way I see it, you can set up a page where you keep all your links, such as book lists or tools you use and do a short write-up for each.

You could include the links in episode description too, especially if you talked about the product during the show. Or you could post a blog article, a product review with links, offers and discounts to follow.

All of these ideas are nothing new, and for years internet marketers have been using them to make money. One thing to keep in mind is that you will need to develop significant traffic to your website. If you get 1,000 views a month, it would be difficult to make a living from affiliate marketing.

On the other hand, if you grow it to several hundred thousand, it's a different game. Remember, just like with everything else, it takes time to build up the infrastructure, and it may take you a while until you start making money with affiliate marketing.

Other ideas

Some other ideas to incorporate affiliate marketing into your podcast business could be a newsletter. It takes time to build up a mailing list, but once you get a significant number of subscribers, every now and then you could include a 'deal' in your newsletter with a link to a product. Another way could be to post offers and recommendations on your social channels. Although, with both newsletters and social media, I would be careful—people sense when you are trying to sell something, and it may backfire.

I view the newsletter and social media as a means of building a community and developing a relationship with listeners, not as a sales funnel. But, it's an option to consider, and a lot of people do just that.

A good way to promote affiliate links is to offer a free eBook or course to people. That's what a lot of YouTube[161] channel authors are doing. By offering free tutorials, they make money if someone buys the products through their link. I don't need to say that it takes a lot of upfront work to do that, but once your material is out there, it can make you money without additional work.

So, an affiliate model could look like this: You run a podcast for graphic designers and develop a mini-course about logo design. On your podcast, you advertise that course as a free tool for listeners. Once they access it, during the course you recommend various tools that will help with logo design: these are affiliate links. When someone buys a product with the link, you make money. It's one of many options, and I hope that if you decide to try affiliate marketing, you will do it in an honest way.

Okay, so where can you find some affiliate marketing offerings? Pretty much everywhere. Most online companies that offer services, software or products offer some affiliate partnership. Commission Junction[162] is one of the most popular for digital products. They offer courses, e-books, software that you can promote in many different niches.

One that could work for podcasters is Audible Affiliate[163] as audiobooks fall not too far away from podcasts. Audible offers incentives for sign-ups as well as sales through a link promoted with your name. I see Audible offers on most podcasting websites, so it must work for them.

Let's not forget about the biggest of all, Amazon Associates.[164] When you sign up for the Amazon affiliate service, you can offer any product they sell and earn a small commission if people buy through your link. Amazon makes sense for physical products, such as books, audio equipment and everything in between. It's a number one affiliate destination for a lot of internet entrepreneurs.

If you don't see the offering for a product that could be a perfect match for your podcast and listeners, just ask the owners directly. Every business is built on sales, and every business owner wants more sales. If you offer help with that, there will be a few who refuse. Don't get discouraged if it's slow in the beginning; it all takes time and patience. Remember, most people overestimate what they can do in a year, but underestimate what they can do in five.

---

158 Smart Passive Income (*https://www.smartpassiveincome.com*)
159 Entrepreneur on Fire (*http://www.eofire.com*)
160 Grammarly (*https://www.grammarly.com*)
161 YouTube (*n 18*)
162 Commission Junction (*http://www.cj.com*)
163 Audible Affiliate (*http://www.audible.co.uk/uk-affiliate-intro*)
164 Amazon Associates (*https://affiliate-program.amazon.com*)

STORE

Merchandise is the backbone of most entertainment businesses. Music, movies, games, they all make a lot more selling merchandise or licensing than on actual content. I'm not saying it's right or wrong, it's just the way it is, so you may as well learn how to use it to your advantage. Fans want to support their idols, and they do it by listening to their, in your case, podcasts and by buying merchandise.

Merch is also a way to create an identity within the community. We wear particular brands because we want to be associated with the tribe. It doesn't matter if it's a t-shirt with your favourite sports team, music band or clothing company. The goal is always the same, to announce to the world 'this is who I am, is there anyone else just like that?'

We tend to think it stops after high school, that we grow out of that kind of thinking. But brands of electronics you use, clothes you wear, programs you watch, and podcasts you listen to mean something too. We belong to tribes, we always will.

When you start a podcast and begin building a community, sooner or later, people will ask about merchandise. They do it all the time with *Casefile*. You're going to buy a coffee mug anyway, so why not support your favourite show at the same time? I don't need to add that merchandise can add another revenue stream that will keep your show going. It's a clear win-win for both you and your listeners.

To be clear, I'm not an expert on setting up a store or running an elaborate merchandise strategy. For *Casefile* it is a bit too early for that. As I'm typing these words, we still don't have a store on our website, and we've only run one Teespring[165] campaign last year, with mediocre results. We often talk about setting something up, but the lack of time and running the show means that it is not a priority right now. We have ideas for the future, but that's what they are at the moment: ideas.

This chapter is going to be a short one, and for beginners only. I'm not going to dive deep into logistics of having a brand, frankly because I don't know how it works. But, I want to show you how you can still set up a store, with items bearing your podcast's logo, without any upfront costs or inventory. It's not an ideal solution, but it's something that will help you test the waters of merchandise, and hopefully be the first step in having branded products in the future.

Thanks to the internet, there are many solutions and platforms to test out merch ideas. Some better than others, but all of them work in a similar manner. You upload the design—it can be anything you want—and when someone buys a product with your design, you earn a commission: royalty.

Many designers make it one of their revenue streams for passive income, producing designs for all kinds of occasions and holidays. For you, it will be a little bit different as you are not looking at appealing to anyone except your core audience, and once you develop a community it's much easier to market the products.

Let's start with few services that I used in the past.

CAFEPRESS, ZAZZLE, REDBUBBLE, SPREADSHIRT

Two years ago, my wife and I were trying to find ideas for the next venture. What to do after we left our full-time jobs. She is a designer, so we wanted to try selling designs and develop a passive income stream. Word of advice, don't believe the 'gurus' on the internet. There is no such thing as 'easy' or 'passive' income. We were experimenting with a few things when we found online stores for designers. The way they work is you upload the design, select the items, promote them and earn money when someone buys the product. No upfront money, no inventory, no logistics. Because she is an excellent designer, we decided to give it a go and tried a few platforms.

CafePress

CafePress[166] is an online gift shop with hundreds of items to choose from.

They have a 'base price' for each product, and you set a mark-up on top of it. However, in their marketplace they use retail price, and you can't go above it. So, for a t-shirt base price is $20. If you set up a store you can use your own mark-up, such as $5, they also will take transaction fees from that. When someone buys from marketplace you earn 10% commission, so on a $20 t-shirt, you make $2.

Zazzle
Similar to CafePress, Zazzle[167] is an online gift store where you upload designs and can set up your shop. They also have hundreds of products to choose from. The royalties start from 5%, which is a default, with 15% for 'high-value' items. You can set the royalties yourself.

RedBubble[168]
The online gift store is destined for artists rather than designers. You will find here intricate drawings and artwork rather than slogans or simple logos. The logistics are similar to other shops but with a mark-up default set at 20% above the base price of the item.

Spreadshirt
Spreadshirt's[169] focus is on t-shirts. However, you can print your designs on other items too. It works the same way as other platforms, but instead of mark-up, you set the price of the design itself, which is then added to the base price of the item. The price you set is between 0–10 British Pounds.

These are just four that I used in the past. I'm sure there are plenty of other platforms and websites that work in a similar way, and like the saying goes, 'Google is your friend'. If you were thinking of setting up a store for your podcast, I wouldn't recommend going with any of these solutions. They work on volume, and the margins are small. We sold a couple of t-shirts, and after transaction fees, we were left with a couple of dollars in profit. Unless you are a designer who can produce hundreds of graphics, you will not make a lot of money.

Let's say you sell 200 t-shirts with your design. I doubt that you would make over $700, and that's pushing it. Producing a podcast will be your top priority, and unless you have a full-time designer working for you, I would look somewhere else.

PRINTIFY, MERCHIFY, AMAZON MERCH

Another solution, one that gives you a bit more control, is having a store on a website, but with outsourced manufacturing and logistics. There are a few online companies that can help you with that. Let's start with Shopify.

Shopify

Shopify[170] is an e-commerce platform that allows you to set up a store, handle inventory, fulfil orders and track sales. It's one of the most popular ones out there. Basic Shopify account starts at $29 per month. You will need them if you want to sell products online. They offer a free fourteen days trial.

Merchify/Printify

Once you have signed up for a Shopify account, you will need an inventory. Both Printify[171] and Merchify[172] work in the same way; they take care of products and logistics. It operates in the same way as other marketplace design platforms. You choose a product, upload the design and set the price. There are no restrictions on how high you can charge for the product in the store. You will need to take the base price of the item and shipping costs into consideration. If you wish to try one of these, read their FAQ pages and choose the one that works for you.

For a while, we wanted to try it with *Casefile*, but we heard mixed opinions on running a store in such a way and decided to leave that idea on the shelf for now. The mixed reviews were about the quality of products and the printing process. It's all hearsay, as I haven't tried it, so I would recommend doing proper research before you commit to one of these options.

Amazon Merch

Amazon tries to break into merchandise space too. They started a venture called Amazon Merch,[173] and I heard good things about it. However, right now you will need an invitation to start selling there. We requested the invite months ago and still haven't heard anything from them. I would watch this space, though, and keep it bookmarked. Amazon is one of the biggest marketplaces online, and if they offer a good deal on merch, it could be a perfect solution for a no-inventory setup.

Teespring

Teespring is the solution we used last year and will probably use in the future. They focus on t-shirts. However, they also offer other products such as tote bags or mugs. Instead of setting up a store, you launch a campaign that runs for a limited time. You set campaign goals, upload the designs and select items you want to sell. After the campaign ends, the products are shipped to customers. Teespring takes care of logistics and returns, so you don't need to hold any inventory.

From all the mentioned options, Teespring has the best margins, and you can make the largest profit with them. The only thing you need to take care of is marketing to your listeners, which is also the hardest part!

One other option that Teespring has is that you can set campaigns on repeat mode, so in reality you have an ongoing store all the time. However, to receive the products, customers must wait until the end of each campaign.

Teespring works best with limited items and limited time, which adds to the urgency and helps in making sales. It's not the perfect solution, but in my opinion, it is the best of the ones I mentioned. Products are high quality, prints look good, and so far everyone has been happy with what they received.

Like I said before, merchandise is something that you should consider, once your show is gaining traction. For now, I offer options for a beginner. We haven't been offered a merchandise deal yet, so I can't advise you on that. Maybe, if things go well, I will be writing how to tackle that issue in the next edition of this book.

> **NOVEMBER 2019 UPDATE**
>
> For a couple of years we did run a Teespring merch store and people enjoyed the designs. However, the problem was in shipping costs, which could be as much as the item. Only recently we switched to RedBubble, which offered lower shipping. We now offer designs in an online store that can be accessed from our website.

PHYSICAL PRODUCTS

I know that merchandise takes the format of a physical product, however in this paragraph I wanted to talk more about a 'special' kind of a product. Let's be honest, t-shirts, stickers, mugs are standard products when it comes to merchandise, everyone starts there. But developing a store offers a lot of exciting opportunities to try out; you just need to have a viable idea.

I'm not going to give you a blueprint for that: there are too many variables depending on the nature of your show. You can try to develop a card game with the help of sites such as Game Crafter,[174] or you could start a membership mystery box, similar to Hunt a Killer.[175] Know your audience, ask what they would like to have and then develop the product to satisfy their needs. Going the other way around rarely works, and you don't want to end up with something that no one wants to buy, after months of planning and labour.

Other ideas? Boards games, books, CDs (anyone still buy them?), vinyl, posters. Yes, selling a physical product is a tough task, especially when you consider manufacturing and logistics. But you could crowdfund it and get the support from your fans first. It could be the next step from a branded mug or a t-shirt.

DIGITAL PRODUCTS

Last but not least are digital products. The most beautiful thing about digital is that you don't need an inventory to reach a lot of people. It takes a lot of upfront work to develop the product, but once it is ready, that's it. Apart from support and maintenance, you don't need to worry about much else. So, what can you sell?

Again, it depends on your show and your listeners. As part of *Casefile* Patreon campaign, we release designs of our scripts as well as an e-magazine. We can also sell them as archives to non-patrons. If you run a non-scripted show, then the same kind of product would not make much sense, so being aware of your brand and audience is the key.

You can develop online courses, e-books, guides, apps, video games, movies, membership groups, just to name a few. Whatever you want to do, ask your listeners if that's something they want or need. Don't make something just for the sake of making money. Offer something of value, something that you would buy yourself.

---

165 Teespring (*https://teespring.com/en-GB*)
166 Cafepress (*http://www.cafepress.co.uk*)
167 Zazzle (*https://www.zazzle.co.uk*)
168 RedBubble (*http://www.redbubble.com*)
169 Spreadshirt (*https://www.spreadshirt.co.uk*)
170 Shopify (*https://www.shopify.co.uk*)
171 Merchify (*https://www.merchify.com*)
172 Printify (*https://printifyapp.com*)
173 Amazon Merch (*https://merch.amazon.com/landing*)
174 Game Crafter (*https://www.thegamecrafter.com*)
175 Hunt a Killer (*https://www.huntakiller.com*)

DONATIONS

The idea of supporting artists isn't new. You can do it by buying merchandise, going to live events, supporting their sponsors. However, online crowdfunding is a new concept that is changing the rules of the game. Instead of having one rich patron that pays the living costs, the artist can now have thousands of fans, who—by donating a small amount of money—support the project together.

Asking your listeners for donations is not an easy thing to do. It changes the dynamic of the relationship, and it adds responsibility to your work. Before donations, you could stop anytime you wanted (within your sponsorship terms), but by asking fans for the monetary support, you made a promise. Every one of us can spend money any way we want. If someone chooses to give you theirs, you must offer something in return, something of value. If you are lucky, then most will only expect you to carry on with the podcast: to grow it, to improve it, to create more of it.

To me, the idea of crowdfunding is fantastic. You can cut out the middleman and speak directly to fans. You can ask for their opinion, check with them before making a big decision; make it worth their time and money. You hear more and more about the projects that received more than enough funds to realise the idea. Only a few days ago I read a post from an entrepreneur who created a board game[176] with a $10k goal on Kickstarter;[177] in two weeks he reached almost $200k. He is not the only one, people recognise the passion and are willing to support it no matter what. But, should you ask fans for donations?

From the early days of *Casefile* I wanted to start crowdfunding, the idea was to start small and grow it with time; to have enough funds and to keep the show running. Last year we decided to go with sponsors only and see if the business model would work. The idea was to keep the show free for everyone, and besides that, running a crowdfunding campaign takes time and effort. We wanted to focus on producing the show.

As I mentioned before, after a few months we realised that sponsorship is tricky and not as easy as it sounds. After a few cancellations with advertisers and the long time it takes to receive the money from the ads, we decided to start a Patreon[178] account. So far we have had incredible support, and we keep improving the campaign with each day.

After looking back, my advice would be to start early with the backing. Maybe not after the first episode, but once you know that you want to produce the show for the foreseeable future, there is no harm in asking for support. We had people asking if they can donate before we even started on our crowdfunding path!

The key is in the balance. If you rely entirely on sponsorship, you put the future of the show in the hands of a few advertisers that can end the contract whenever they want. If you work only towards crowdfunding, you may sound desperate to some and turn people away. However, if you treat donations as another source of revenue that helps your podcast, it will make the campaign less stressful to run. Even if it takes months to get rolling, other income streams will cover you.

Let's not forget the idea I mentioned before, the *1,000 True Fans*[179] post by Kevin Kelly. If you can find a 1,000 people who are willing to spend $100 a year on your art, you will have a salary of $100k doing something that you love. I think we all should be moving towards that model. What is better than having true fans that are willing to support you along your journey?

Before you decide to move on with crowdfunding, let's have a look at a few platforms that can help to fund a podcast.

PATREON

Patreon must be the most popular platform for crowdfunding out there, especially when talking about monthly support. There, you will find musicians, video creators, streamers, among other creators. I don't have to add that it is the perfect place for podcasters, given the nature of the medium.

So, how does it work? You create an account on Patreon and build a campaign. You can add the video explaining why you have chosen to go down that route and do a write-up about your show: how it all started, info about the team and what your plans are for the future. The more details on the main page, the better. You should also pay attention to the visuals. Edit your posts, make the artwork presentable, and proofread the text. Don't skimp on the work, show that you are a professional and you respect the time and money of your potential supporters.

Next are the tiers for patrons. You can create many different levels of support or have one 'pay whatever you wish'. I've seen successful accounts with elaborate support systems from $1 to $50 per month pulling a few thousand pledges per month. I've also seen accounts where podcasters had only one tier of $5 per month with thousands of patrons supporting them. I don't think there is a perfect answer or strategy. Decide on one, wait for some time, and adjust it if you need to. I prefer to have a choice, so we decided on three tiers. We decided to give it three months and review the strategy after that period.

Of course, the first thing that you should keep in mind is the Patreon awards. These are perks that you will offer to supporters. I don't see it as sales, more as appreciation gifts for those who choose to help you out. Each tier should have some perks as an incentive for patrons. These can be whatever you wish. A special message, live Ask-Me-Anything sessions, special episodes, discounts on merchandise. It's best to know the audience and know what they would appreciate.

If you think that people should give you money just because they listen to your podcast, then you will be disappointed. People don't want to pay for things that are free; you should offer something extra to validate the expense, even a small gesture will often be more than enough. Never take your listeners, or their support, for granted. I know that I'm repeating myself, but remember that they can change to another podcast with a click of a button. Respect that they choose to spend valuable time with you.

PAYPAL BUTTON

Another option is to include a PayPal[180] button on your website for one-time donations. I have seen some podcasters do it. Therefore, it must work for them. Myself, I'm not convinced about that solution. Yes, it may seem better than Patreon as you will receive the money straight to your PayPal account, cutting out the other platforms and fees, but there is no incentive for the support. You pay the money, and that's it, no reward. Unless, of course, you will set something up on your website.

Another thing is that donating via PayPal is a lonely endeavour. You must remember that podcasting is about the community, and crowdfunding is about community too. On platforms such as Patreon, your supporters can chat with others, comment on posts and engage with one another. It makes it worth paying these few dollars per month. With a PayPal button, you are not offering that, not to mention that on crowdfunding platforms you also have a direct contact with your supporters and can answer their questions.

As you can see, I'm not keen on the PayPal button idea. By all means, try it, and it may work for you. Everyone is different, every podcast is different, and every fan is different. What works for us may not work for you and vice versa. But crowdfunding or not, I urge you to remember to put the community at the heart of your show. Without listeners, you are just a person talking to a microphone.

KICKSTARTER

Kickstarter must be the biggest and best-known crowdfunding platform out there. So many projects have been funded through the platform, it's hard to count them all. When people sense passion, they support it. Of course, Kickstarter may make a bit less sense for a podcaster than, let's say, Patreon. On Kickstarter, you run campaigns with a time limit, 30 days for example. With Patreon you get monthly subscriptions to support you.

It doesn't mean you should dismiss the platform straight away. It could work if, for example, you are planning on releasing a seasonal podcast. Or maybe you could plan a 'special' mini-series on top of the normal schedule and, to cover additional costs, you could run a Kickstarter campaign. The possibilities are endless. You could come up with a product, an app or a book. Kickstarter could allow you to take time off work if needed, to have peace of mind while you are working out the logistics. With *Casefile* we may use it someday, who knows?

Crowdfunding is an excellent way to get support from people who are not looking at hard ROI, like advertisers or investors. They just want to keep you producing the podcast they love. Kickstarter and Patreon are not the only ones out there, just Google 'crowdfunding platform' to check the others and see which one could work best for you. Indiegogo[181] and GoFundMe[182] also have many successful stories. The platforms don't matter: it's about the people who help to fund your dream.

---

176 Kickstarter Tortuga (*https://www.kickstarter.com/projects/travishancock/tortuga-1667-a-pirate-game-of-mutiny-plunder-and-d*)
177 Kickstarter (*https://www.kickstarter.com*)
178 Patreon (*n 123*)
179 Kevin Kelly – 1000 True Fans (*n 129*)
180 PayPal (*https://www.paypal.com/gb/home*)
181 Indiegogo (*https://www.indiegogo.com*)
182 GoFundMe (*https://uk.gofundme.com*)

PAYWALL

In the last chapter about monetising a podcast, I want to talk about paid content. For most parts, podcasts are free for anyone who wants to listen. They are not free to make or host, but listeners do not have to pay to hear the show. Personally, I do like the idea of providing value to people and receiving back only when I deserve it. However, that's not always sustainable, or smart business-wise.

Producing high-quality audio drama can cost a lot of money. When I am talking about hiring scriptwriters and actors, production and post-production, costs can quickly skyrocket into thousands of dollars. It's not as expensive as producing a movie or a video game, but as spoken word becomes more familiar, with time, more money will circulate in the industry.

As you have already learnt, many models can sustain that kind of endeavour: sponsorship, donations, merchandise, to name a few. All of these are means of keeping your show free and available to everyone. But, maybe at some point in the future, you will decide to record an 'extra' episode or season. Maybe even start a whole new show as premium content. If you don't want to go through securing sponsorship or crowdfunding again, you may choose a paid content route. What is that?

Well, there is not much philosophy there. Let's say episode X of your show is free to listen to everyone, but episode Y costs 0.99 cents to download. A standard pay-to-play model. These models are becoming a way to consume content, with the most popular, Netflix[183] and Amazon,[184] taking charge in on-demand streaming. There are plenty of smaller platforms targeting a niche, such as Shudder[185] for horror fans. Video games are slowly following suit, and it's a matter of time that paid streaming for podcasts will take its market share.

For now, most podcasts are free, but there are already a few options out there and more than a few people who want to monetise the popularity of the medium. What the trend tends to be is that, by paying money, you will get ad-free, better quality podcasts: a professional production and more value than you would get with a free version. I think it's a tough sell. People don't tend to pay for things that were free in the first place. But time will tell, everything can change in an instant.

First, let's have a look at some of the services out there.

Howl[186]

Howl is a paid service that offers over 150 hours of original mini-series as well as over 120 comedy albums from top comedians. People can sign up for a free trial, and after that, it works out as $4.99/month or $44.99/year. The app works both on Android and IOS.

Stitcher Premium

Similar to Howl, they offer ad-free listening, however, if you incorporate adverts into your show, they will still be there. On top of that, members get access to bonus episodes and original series developed for the platform, as well as comedy albums. It costs $4.99/month or $34.99/year.

Recent news from 2016 is that Midroll—one of the biggest podcast advertising networks—not only acquired Stitcher[187] but is also a parent company of Howl. I think it will be just a matter of time before Howl and Stitcher Premium become one service.

How can you get your podcast on one of these platforms? Right now the best shot is to become so famous that they come to you and present you the offer. Usually, the offer will be for bonus series exclusive for their platform, bonus episodes or a whole new podcast. The contract should include some money in advance as well as a percentage of sales from sign-ups to the platform.

If you decide to go this way you can always try MyLibsyn. MyLibsyn is a subscription management service that helps you to distribute paid content.

You can offer videos, documents, bonus episodes, back catalogue. The system allows you to set custom plans, develop an app and track the statistics. The revenue share is split 50/50 with Libsyn company, however, once you reach a significant number of downloads your share can grow to as high as 70/30. All the billing and customer support is handled by the service. That option means that you can start with paid content from day one and, for the most part, you are in charge of what you are producing.

If you want to have 100% control over how you handle pay-to-play, there are plenty of shows that sell seasonal passes or yearly memberships for their fans. You can run it as an e-commerce store with direct links to your episodes, bonus materials and other perks. The possibilities are limitless.

I think it's a good idea to secure funds for production and show development and, if you have a big enough audience, only a small percentage will suffice to support you along the way.

NOVEMBER 2019 UPDATE

Netflix-for-podcasts is a phrase that gets repeated very often and many have tried and are still trying to make it work.

Exclusive 'behind the paywall' podcasts are now a thing and the trend will continue to go in that direction. We have been offered that in the past and refused. It will be interesting to see how the listenership develops along these kinds of services. One thing that I personally learnt is that it is very difficult to convince people to pay for something that was once free. Even if they don't like the ads that come with 'free' stuff.

---

183 Netflix (*https://www.netflix.com*)
184 Amazon (*n 67*)
185 Shudder (*http://www.shudder.com*)
186 Howl (*http://lp.howl.fm/welcome*)
187 Midroll acquires Stitcher (*http://www.stitcher.com/blog/?p=1734*)

PART IV

Growing Your Podcast

In the last part of the book I want to discuss what happens when you 'hit it big time' in the podcasting world. I don't mean superstar level like Joe Rogan,[188] but I'm still talking about a significant number.

Casefile hovers around Top 50 on the U.S. iTunes most of the times, sometimes falling to seventies, sometimes climbing as high as thirties/forties, depending on the week. Considering that there must be hundreds of thousands of podcasts, being in the Top 50, and staying there, is a proverbial 'success'. We never planned for it, but it happened. The show grew from thousands of downloads to tens of thousands to hundreds of thousands, and it has had a steady growth ever since.

Why did it happen to us? As I said as I presented you my theory in the past chapters, it was a combination of multiple variables. One thing is sure, once you reach a bigger audience, the opportunities you get are very different. I don't claim that we are going to stay so popular: I can't guarantee it. I know that we will try to innovate and produce good content, that's about it. I cannot guarantee that you will get the same results in the similar period as *Casefile*. Everyone is different and every situation is unique.

It's not a blueprint. It's not a step-by-step guide to success. If someone tries to sell you something like that, be suspicious. Selling a dream usually turns out to be exactly that, a dream.

But! There are many things that I learnt during my adventure with *Casefile*, and things that only appeared when we joined the ranks of successful podcasts. These are, for the most part, taken from direct experience so may not be an industry standard or the way it always works, but I wanted to present an idea of what may happen if you taste success and how you can get ready for it. No, you won't be sitting on the beach sipping cocktails; no, you won't be cruising in sports cars in expensive clothes. Or maybe you will, who knows?

We are still at the beginning of the journey. Treat it as a work in progress, not a definite guide. One of many steps you will need to take. There will be more responsibility, more work, higher costs, legal issues, hiring people and on and on. Don't think it will happen in a linear manner either. Writing it on paper may look like that, like any business plan. However, if you have ever run a business, you know that it's never structured or linear. It's chaos, with multiple issues coming up all at once. Be ready, be prepared and plan for it. Cause even if you don't, it may still happen.

---

188 Joe Rogan Experience (*n 7*)

OFFERS

The minute you start hitting significant download numbers, you will start getting offers from all over the place, from people you don't know and have never met. Just like A&R guys in the music industry, podcasting world has 'agents' that scout the space looking for new talent. As we all know, manufactured product works, but the authentic content always wins in the long run and agencies understand that. To have a 'star' podcast on their books gives them leverage, prestige and negotiating power with advertisers and, of course, when they sense the potential to make money they will try to recruit you as fast as possible.

You should think through each offer, check with a professional on the side and sleep on the final decision. Don't be swayed by the numbers or the friendly calls: each person that talks to you has an agenda, a target and a boss they answer to. They may want to help, but without big download numbers they wouldn't be talking to you. There is nothing wrong with that; you should look for win-win scenarios, when everyone gets what they want and more. Apart from that, once your show gets big enough, it will require extra help to push it to the next level.

I'm assuming that you don't know people in the merchandise, music, film, book and other industries. Well, these people do, that's their job. They can connect you with the right services and personnel. Be cautious but open. You don't have to agree to anything after a meeting, and until you sign a contract, you don't owe anything to anyone.

What kind of offers can you expect?

TV deal

At the time of writing this paragraph, it seems like turning podcasts into TV series is the latest trend. Production companies that will present you with a deal for a TV series may approach you. I'm getting ahead of myself here. More than likely you will be offered something called a shopping agreement.

Shopping agreement means that a production company will develop what is called a sizzle reel based on your show and will pitch it to television networks trying to secure a 'green light' for a pilot. You won't get paid at this point, and you will sign off the right to pitch TV/film/whatever else for a set period. You are giving the production company a time to 'shop it around'.

If you are lucky enough and your show gets a 'green-light' for a pilot, then depending on negotiation you will either help during the production and get paid for that, or just feature as the creator of the show in the credits. I don't have to say that TV is an entirely different game with many rules and hoops to jump through. When I worked at the movie studio I saw how involved film production is. TV is similar. You are not talking thousands of dollars anymore, but hundreds of thousands, or millions. It's rare to get the idea green-lit and even more unusual to get picked up for a season, almost impossible to stay on the air.

However, it can happen, you just need a bit of luck. But for productions such as TV, you will most likely have to give up a good chunk of creative control over the content. It all depends on your priorities and principles.

Regarding money, a TV deal means getting more cash than you would from a podcast. A lot more. That's why it is so hard to get into the game. With podcasts, it is just you and maybe a couple of other people. With TV or film production it's at a minimum hundreds of individuals, everyone with a different opinion. And, as you can imagine, the chances of producing something good are slim.

Depending on the nature of a show, you can always try to go with independent filmmakers and smaller productions. It has its pros and cons, like everything else. Read the contract and be aware of what you are signing.

Exclusivity

At some point, you may get offers with 'exclusive' contracts, meaning that once you sign with one entity, you agree only to use their services. The terms of the agreement may include production, publishing, advertising and so on. Once you have a popular podcast, people want to get you under their wings, and they don't like to share.

Why would you ever agree to something like that? You will either get an offer with a significant advance or excellent conditions. How does the advance works? Remember when I showed you how sponsorship works? That you will wait around four to five months for your first checks to come through the post? Well, money advance comes to the rescue! Let's take an example of exclusivity with a podcast advertising network.

They offer you an exclusive, twelve month contract with an advance of $100k and a revenue split share of 70/30. You will get half at the moment of signing the agreement and the other half at the end of an agreed date. It means that you don't have to wait until sponsor checks come in. However, the revenue from the ads will have to offset the advance first. So your 70% from sponsors will have to repay the $100k advance, and only then will you start earning from the ads.

If you have two ads per episode, each worth $5k, with four episodes a month:

2 × 5 × 4 = $40k/month
0.7 (your cut) × 40k = 28k

It will take you around three to four months to work back the advancement. After that, you will be netting 28k/month, albeit with a delay of few weeks.

These numbers are of course made up; you will need to have a serious podcast to get $10k worth of ads per episode, as well as $100k advancement. Plus there is also a matter of hosting. Once you sign an 'exclusive' contract you may be offered 'free' hosting as a part of a service. It's only free on paper, because, if you go with it, it will diminish your revenue to 60/40 or even 50/50.

And if we calculate the numbers again: 0.5 × 40k = 20k. Suddenly, it takes you five months to work back the advance. You may go with your own hosting, but at this point you will be attracting big download numbers, meaning the show will require significant bandwidth, and that's not cheap. So, you may be getting an advancement of $100k, but if hosting costs you $10k/month, you better save something on the side for that.

Remember, when you approach a hosting company and tell them that you signed an exclusive contract with someone else, they won't offer you a deal. Most hosting companies also provide advertising services, and if you have a big podcast, they will want to get a 'slice of the pie' too. Otherwise, they host your show, and someone else gets the revenue.

These are hypothetical situations, but nevertheless, you need to be wary of these things. Once bigger offers enter the game, it's not as easy as it was in the beginning. Don't sign anything blindly and consider all the options. The advance may sound sweet at first sight, but there are always conditions to be met. Otherwise, what stops you from cashing the money and not producing the content?

Every business protects itself; that goes for you as much as for other parties. Therefore, once again, I would recommend looking for win-win scenarios and getting professional help.

Long-term deals

Another offer that can appear once you get good download numbers is a long-term deal with advertisers. Instead of buying one or two spots, advertisers may try to buy an inventory for six months or even a whole year. It doesn't mean every episode, but many adverts spread throughout the year.

Like I mentioned before, this is not guaranteed, as there is usually a clause that will allow cancelling the contract within an agreed period. If you keep providing excellent service, there shouldn't be any surprises, but be ready nevertheless.

Long-term deals will usually be negotiated on a flat-rate basis, and because of a bulk buy, they will also offer a discount. Let's say it worked out as $2,000 per ad, but halfway through the year you get a massive jump in download numbers, and you start charging other sponsors $6,000 per slot. Because you signed a long-term contract, you won't be able to raise the price and are stuck with whatever you negotiated in the beginning. So, it is a question of relative comfort in knowing what you will get or trying your luck to secure something new each week. There is always an option to cancel the deal, but I doubt it will look good and you may hurt your reputation.

Otherwise, if you will consistently overdeliver throughout the year, then after the contract ends you can always try to negotiate a higher rate for the new one.

Premium content

In the last chapter, I talked about creating pay-for-play content. You can do it yourself, but when a podcast gains popularity, you may get offers for producing premium content. On top of your regular show, you may be asked to produce a mini-series, a few extra episodes, even a new podcast series, and all of that will be hidden behind a paywall. The offer will usually present money advancement and a royalty scheme. Not only will you get paid up front, but you will also earn a commission every time someone signs up to the paid service through your link. More than likely, though, you will have to work back the advance first.

This kind of an offer can be a great additional revenue source as well as an opportunity to produce something different. Of course, the biggest issue will be time. So, for example, it would be difficult for our team to do something like that: we are still trying to keep up with the schedule of regular *Casefile* episodes. Until something changes, it is highly improbable that we will find extra time to work on premium content.

However, if you ever find yourself in a situation where working on a podcast is your primary source of income, that's amazing. I would then recommend getting additional projects, especially when the offer is attractive enough.

Authors, filmmakers, creatives

When you start gaining popularity and growing an audience, you will start receiving a lot of 'invites' from writers, filmmakers and other people in the creative space. The emails will almost always look similar: 'I like your show. I created something. Can you promote my product?' Unless it is someone that you know, I would probably ignore requests like that.

I mean, take *Casefile* for example, we receive a lot of emails from creators stating that they love our show, that they created something in the true crime genre, be it a film or a book, and they ask if we could interview them about their product. First of all, they are not offering anything of value in return and second... if they listened to the show, they would know that we don't do interviews! As much as we like to help out and collaborate with people, you can spot these kinds of 'template' emails from a mile. This is not a rant or anything, just a friendly warning.

Once you get a bit of what others perceive as 'success', you will get a lot of requests for favours. In the beginning, it may look harmless and even surprising that so many people are reaching out to you. These emails will not lead to anything and are a huge time sucker, time that you could spend on developing the podcast.

I want to make it clear that these are not the only offers you may get. There are plenty of other opportunities in merchandise, licensing, voice work. I'm writing this guide based on the personal experience I have had so far. I'm sure that, with time, we will learn and see more than I presented to you here. Hopefully, I will get to share that too.

LEGAL

Once you start growing a podcast and, what is more important, making money from it, it is no longer a hobby. It becomes a business with staff, expenses, costs, revenue and accounting. Suddenly, something that seemed like a fun project to do in spare afternoons becomes a complicated venture. You can't avoid things like finances and contracts anymore; you will need to set up a structure.

A structure will help to protect your intellectual property as well as grow the podcast. The seriousness of it all will come with time, and this part of the guide deals with what happens when you reach that time. Don't get me wrong, it's still fun and games, but with a bigger check and a broader audience comes extra work and challenges that you will need to address. It's different running a podcast that gets millions of downloads per month versus a couple of hundred. I guess what I'm trying to say is, don't stress about it when you start, but be ready and be prepared. It's similar to martial arts training: apart from the health benefits most people don't train with the aim of walking around and beating others up. They train to be ready if the situation requires action, and that gives them comfort and peace of mind.

Starting limited liability company
First thing would be to start a limited liability company (please check business laws of your own country first). Once the podcast is generating revenue, you will need to declare it with your government. You may do it as a sole trader, and when it's still a hobby, you can operate as self-employed without too many worries.

However, if you are planning on signing deals, you better get some protection. To cut it short, if you are operating as a sole trader, you are liable for everything that you do; if you get sued, you can lose personal belongings. Limited liability protects you from that. Yes, your podcast as a business can go bankrupt, but you as a person are not liable for that. So a contract is with others and the company, the podcast, and not you.

It is just the simplest explanation I could write, but the recommendation would be to register as a company once you join the 'big leagues'. It's not a complicated process, depending on the country you reside in, and it will alleviate a lot of future headaches.

> *Quick tip*
> I am not a business advisor, and the suggestion is based on my business experience in the UK. Before making a decision, please make sure you consult with a professional and understand the business laws of your country.

Accounting

I showed you that the revenue from podcasting is not as straightforward as getting a job and, more than likely, it will involve multiple revenue streams. Growing a podcast as a business will also require help, so you may want to hire a producer, researcher, social media manager, agent and others. That involves setting aside money for expenses. On top of that, you will incur costs, such as recording equipment, podcast hosting services, website hosting services, website maintenance, mailing list fees, legal fees, graphic design costs, to name a few.

In the beginning, you can do it all yourself, but as time passes, you will find yourself spending a lot more time on spreadsheets. Without proper accounting, you may not realise that you are going into debt, even though your show is more popular than ever. At this point, getting help from a professional would be viable. You don't want the team to argue and leave because of money. You don't want the hosting company to cut services because you are behind on the payments and still a few months away from another sponsor check.

Get the finances under control, and you can spend the time on the important things, creating the best podcast out there. And don't forget about the taxes.

Lawyers

Should you pay for a lawyer? Given that it's only a podcast? If you are looking at signing contracts that may be worth tens or hundreds of thousands of dollars, then yes. If you are about to sign a TV deal, or licensing deal, or advancement deal, then yes. Any deal should be analysed with a professional at your side. Why? I guarantee that the other party has had legal advice and it is okay to negotiate contracts before signing.

You may think to yourself, 'I don't need to spend hundreds of dollars for a lawyer's advice. I get the gist of it all: it all seems pretty straightforward.' Unless you are a professional and understand every single word that is on the paper, don't sign anything. Have you ever heard the horror stories of artists signing away their rights and going broke? Well, things like that happen. You should always protect your property and your business. If something isn't clear and you do not understand it, ask for an explanation, or ask a lawyer to re-write it.

It may cost some cash up front, but it will create savings and earn you a lot more in the long run. Probably the best choice would be to get a lawyer who specialises in the entertainment industry, though their advice might be quite expensive. Podcasting is still a relatively unregulated industry, and you should take your steps with caution. Don't put your name on something you don't understand.

Contracts

If it's not written down, then it doesn't exist. It is as simple as that. When your podcast becomes a growing business, you will be either writing contracts or reading them. Every contract should be as simple as possible, but covering any potential disputes at the same time. As I always say, it should be a win-win for both parties. Even better, when it comes to negotiation, the party that isn't desperate for the result is always in better position. People can sense desperation, and use it to their advantage.

Don't be swayed by empty promises or money advances, if you sign something that takes away your rights or creative control, money can quickly lose its value. Especially, if you care about what you do. The simplest solution is to always be fair to the other parties; even if the contract falls through, you will walk away knowing that you did the best you could.

Sometimes it is better just to walk away, don't be inclined to sign anything just because it took a lot of time to negotiate. Nothing is guaranteed without the signature, so don't rely on handshakes or conference calls. It's business, so treat other people with respect and professionalism, but in the end you are not there to make friends, but to sign deals that will satisfy both parties. It's a long-term game. Don't make hasty decisions, don't give in to the emotions and don't spread rumours. You never know whom you will meet again on your journey, a few years down the road.

Always try to sign a deal that benefits everyone in a fair way and you will make strong relationships that last a long time.

RESPONSIBILITY

"With great power comes great responsibility." Most know that quote, and even if with podcasting you may not get superpowers, as you grow there will be additional responsibility. Accountability to your fans, team members, sponsors, partners is first on the list. Don't get me wrong, it's still fun, but it's hard to abandon the podcast and schedule at your wish. In the past, you could have deleted your channel, and that's it, most wouldn't notice. When you have commitments, it is more difficult.

This short chapter is a warning: remember where you started and how you got to where you are now. Don't think that you are invincible; people lose interest within a second, especially on the internet. When you get a taste of 'success', it doesn't get easier. You will be putting in more hours, more money and more effort than ever before. There isn't a lot of space at the top of the mountain, and many people want to be there. Some want to take your place by pushing you down and will wait for the smallest misstep. Be true to your mission, work hard and keep overdelivering and you won't lose; but don't forget that you too are now carrying a burden.

Responsibility to yourself
First and foremost, you need to make sure you are still having fun with the show. If you started a podcast to make money, then it will be hard to keep working on it, especially as it takes a lot of time and effort to get some revenue in. Most successful people started podcasts because they want to share ideas and stories. They had something they were passionate about and wanted to find like-minded people; they enjoyed doing it. Once you get popular, you will get a lot of attention, not always positive. You may start to worry about the revenue, costs, numbers, sponsors, content and reviews.

You may get lost in stress and struggle to sit behind the microphone. It will become a chore, a job rather than an adventure.

The primary goal, the one that I always repeat, is that the whole venture should be fun, for the most part. Yes, there will be setbacks and negative comments, but remind yourself that you are doing something you like and it doesn't need to be serious.

Things change, you change every day. In six months you may be in a different place, with different ideas and jobs. Instead of worrying about download numbers or sponsors, enjoy the moment. People seem to like your podcast, that's amazing. Be grateful and try to have fun while doing it.

Responsibility to fans

Once you have a big audience that awaits the podcast, your responsibility is to provide the best content you can, no excuses. Especially when you start crowdfunding, charging for content or selling merchandise. Once money starts rolling in, you may want to relax a bit, take time off, skimp on a few episodes. That's fine; everyone needs to wind down.

When it comes to working, for me, getting paid for podcasting means working harder than I did in the beginning. The quality of content should be paired with the revenue. Don't get lazy just because you had a good year. The year will pass, so build something that can last for a long time.

If there ever is a question of content versus money, content always wins. Look at Disney,[189] you may think that it's the theme parks and merchandise that makes them the most revenue, but without the content and the movies, these products would not be attractive to fans. Content is a gateway to recognition, marketing, sales, products and profits. In the past it may not have mattered as much, but in today's world, you can be almost 100% sure that every product has a cheaper, better, more efficient version. Globalisation allows everyone to join the market, but it also means only the 'cream will rise to the top.'

People have a limited amount of time that they can spend on consuming the content. In the past you only had one TV channel to watch, today there are countless videos on the internet and only the best, most interesting or most controversial win. It's easier to get into the market, but harder than ever to break through the crowd. Don't think the fans won't leave you for a better podcast the minute you start procrastinating, because they will.

It's your responsibility to get your audience engaged, to supply them with interesting stories, to help them escape once they put the headphones on. Otherwise, you are just wasting everybody's time, and time is the most valuable resource we have. For the most part we have the same amount of it.

Paying bills

Another responsibility that you will come across once you get some accomplishment with your podcast is expenses. No longer will your show cost a few dollars for hosting. Depending on what you are producing, expenses will vary, but I can guarantee they will be higher than when you started.

Some shows are more expensive than others, but to keep the quality up and to run the business, you will have expenditures, such as paying your team members, legal advice, accounting services, hosting, web maintenance, design work. One rule says always to pay yourself first, which sounds awesome in theory but sometimes it is impossible to fulfil in practice. If you don't pay your producer or designer, your content suffers, and the audience will notice.

It can get tough, particularly in the early stages of growth. Remember when I told you how sponsorship works? And how long it takes to get the money? Let's assume that your podcast is quite cheap to produce, and overall costs are $1,000 per month. Four episodes x $250. That still adds up to $5,000 of expenses while you are waiting for sponsorship money, assuming it takes around five months to get the checks from podcasting networks. Plus, even if the revenue starts coming in, you still have to pay the costs each month.

And what if your podcast demands high production? What if it's an audio drama with voice actors, music, and professional sound mixing? It can cost a $1,000 minimum to produce an episode, with $10,000 per episode for the most famous dramas.

How do you cover that? It's your responsibility to keep your finger on the pulse of the costs and be ahead of the numbers. It's fun to run a podcast that people enjoy, but it's not pleasant to run a failing business.

> *Quick tip*
> The costs are based on top-quality podcasts with an expensive production process. In the beginning, you won't need to spend anywhere near that amount, so don't get discouraged.

Impressions

Once you start selling slots for advertisement, you make the sales based on impressions the ads will get. I don't need to say that it is always better to overdeliver than to break the promise.

Let's say your last episode was downloaded over 100k times, so you start selling ad slots for 100k impressions. But what if that episode was just a one off? What if the next one falls to 60k downloads? Now you have a problem on your hands and a breach of contract, which can lead to a dispute and a delay in getting paid.

Some episodes will be more popular than others, and for the most part you won't be able to predict which ones. We try to answer these questions and come up with some 'golden' formula. The answers are for the most parts assumptions and pure speculation, so we don't sell the impressions based on that.

Higher download numbers will attract extra attention, but they will always regress to the mean. Your strategy should always be underpromise and overdeliver. Not the other way around.

New ideas

Your ultimate responsibility as a successful podcaster is to keep brainstorming and coming up with new ideas. You may think you have discovered a perfect blueprint for a successful show, but people get bored. They will listen to your show, leave a comment and recommend it to a friend, but then they will move on with their lives, like everybody else. Even if you are number one, you are not special or better than others. You have fifteen minutes in the spotlight, that's all. Soon the spotlight will shine at somebody else, and you will be left alone in the dark. What's the solution?

Don't worry about it too much. Such is life and change is constant. Your worry should be to keep experimenting, delivering the best content you can, each time you release something to the world. Make something different, something interesting, and something exciting. Not everyone will like it, and a lot of people may hate it. That's the whole game. Once you step into the ring, be prepared to get punched a little. The game is not for everyone, that's why most people sit outside the ring, where it's safe.

> **NOVEMBER 2019 UPDATE**
>
> We are fortunate enough that the show continued to grow and still retained the quality that I've always pushed for. Not only did it result in being able to focus on the podcast full-time but also to grow our team.
>
> We had offers from all over the place—TV deals, live event deals, merch, dubbings and more. However, it all takes an incredible amount of time and negotiation and most of it dies at the early stages.
>
> The biggest change for us was starting *Casefile Presents*, a platform where we want to help other podcasters with their shows. We've tried to get this idea off the ground for a long time and finally did that a few months ago.
>
> Besides that, *Casefile* still takes priority as we have a full-on schedule with regular episodes, bonus content for Patreon, plus other projects.
>
> Getting to this point is absolutely incredible. However, we are definitely not chilling on a beach and are working harder than ever, and this won't change in the foreseeable future.
>
> However, I wouldn't have it any other way.

---

189 Disney (*www.disneystore.co.uk*)

THE END

Is it the end or just the beginning? It's both. The end of this guide and beginning of your adventure. Remember, what you learnt in this book is not only the basics that will help you to kick off your podcast, but also guidelines. These are not rules; nothing is set in stone. Over a year ago I didn't know anything about podcasting, and by some dumb luck I ended up working on a quite popular one.

Everything I've learnt so far is on these few pages. Is it a compendium of podcasting knowledge? Absolutely not. These are my experiences, and my perspective on the state of the industry. Your journey will be different; you will meet different people and challenges. I hope that you will persist in the pursuit of quality content and compelling stories.

Podcasting is still a niche medium, and yet radio has been with us for decades. Trends tend to go in circles, and maybe that's why more and more people tune into the spoken word. Combine it with a flexibility and convenience, and you have a perfect way to share ideas.

Looking back at this year, would I do anything different? Probably not. Every mistake we made, every setback we had, they all made us go back at it stronger and with more persistence, and taught us that there will be many setbacks along the way.

As I'm typing these words I haven't left my house yet, and it's already 6 pm. I've edited another episode of *Casefile*, mixed a bit of music and posted something on social media. No excitement, no awards, no glamour, it's just the screen and me. 99% of podcasting work is like that—grind, work, computer screen, typing and tea on the side of the desk. I wouldn't expect anything more, nor would I want anything else. That's the main point of it all; I often ask the Host, "Are we still having fun?" because if we don't then there is no point in any of it.

Money? You can make way more starting a store online or something.

Fame? Not in podcasting, and I won't count on being the next *Serial*.[190] The chances of success are slim, and it takes a lot of work to get it off the ground.

So, why do it at all? Well, why not? It's not binding, you can stop anytime you want, but I warn you, once you catch the podcasting bug, it's not easy to end it, even if it's just a few listeners out there. We all need to feel significant, we all seek validation and podcasting can give you that. First and foremost, have fun.

I look forward to this year; I hope that *Casefile* will continue to deliver quality podcasts to listeners and, last of all, I hope to see your podcast on the charts soon.

There is no better time to start than now, today. Don't overthink it, just do it and enjoy the process. I'll see you on the other side.

Mike

P.S.
If you liked the book, visit my website www.mikemigas.com where I have more content about work, audio and podcasting on my blog. I'm also working on a few online courses that will help podcasters on their journey.

---

190 Serial (*n* 12)

ABOUT THE AUTHOR

Mike Migas is an audio editor, composer and producer. After moving to the UK and completing his studies, he joined the biggest film studio in Europe—Pinewood Film Studios. As a team leader, he worked on several blockbuster movies for Disney, Marvel, Pixar and Star Wars at the International Sound department. After leaving the industry, he focused on working with podcasters and audiobook producers.

Mike currently produces a popular true crime podcast *Casefile* and runs a personal blog at mikemigas.com.

To learn more about *Casefile: True Crime Podcast* visit casefilepodcast.com or *Casefile*'s Facebook, Twitter and Instagram accounts.

INDEX

Symbols

3-1 rule 74
99designs 102
.wav 90

A

absorbers 71
accountability 36, 178
accounting 174, 175, 180
advanced editing 78–80
advertisement 10, 116, 131–137, 181
    ad agency 137
    ads 81, 96, 113, 124, 132, 134–141, 156, 162, 170
    AdSense 141
    AdWords 49, 124
    mid-roll 135, 144
    post-roll 135, 144
    pre-roll 135, 144
affiliations 18, 19, 130, 143
    affiliate marketing 17, 143–146
Amazon Merch 151
amplitude 40
Apple 25, 35, 63, 66, 92, 94, 98, 100, 104, 123
ART19 96–98, 138
artwork 18, 35, 48–50, 92, 98, 100–107, 150, 157
    design 18
    cover art 103
atmospheric pressure 40
Audacity 63, 65
audio 9, 18, 23, 24, 31, 32, 49, 50, 52–66, 76–92, 95, 107, 111, 120, 138, 180
    drama 49, 57, 79, 86–88, 90, 95, 120, 160, 180
    interface 9, 52–56, 59–77
    quality 90
Audioboom 96–97
audiobooks 10, 22, 64, 146
authority 23, 133
Aweber 114

B

bandwidth 91, 95–98, 171
banner 124, 132, 139, 141
Behance 103
blog 4, 20, 49, 121, 131
Blubrry 95, 97–98, 137
blueprint 4–5, 17, 112, 153, 166, 181
booming bass 70
business 5, 11, 17, 21–34, 44, 48–50, 111–118, 122, 129, 132, 141–148, 156, 160, 167, 171, 174–180
Buzzsprout 96, 98

C

Cafepress 149
cables 57–59, 65, 74
   balanced 57–59
   unbalanced 57–58
cancellations 141
Carlin, Dan 7
Casefile i, iii–iv, vi–vii, ix–xi, 3–12,
   17–18, 21–25, 27, 30, 32–34,
   37–39, 45–52, 57, 60–63, 66,
   73, 76–96, 100, 101–125, 131,
   136, 138–139, 144, 148, 148,
   151, 154, 159, 166, 172, 182–184
colour coding 78, 83
communication 21, 39, 109
composing 85
compression 42, 83–84, 88
contract 72, 134–137, 140, 156, 161,
   168–171, 174–176, 181
Convertkit 114
Covey, Stephen 27
CPM 134–135
crowdfunding 155–160, 179
Csikszentmihalyi, Mihaly 22, 38
CTA (call-to-action) 120, 125, 144

D

deadline 37–38, 44
decibel 41
de-esser 69
design 18, 23, 70, 100–104, 143–154,
   175, 180
diffusers 71
digital products 146, 153
directionality 54
distance 41, 67–69, 74
donations 18, 129–130, 155–158, 160

downloads 25, 93–95, 113, 123,
   131–138, 160, 162, 166, 174
Dumas, John Lee 143

E

ear 42, 87
   inner ear 42
   middle ear 42
   outer ear 42
early reflections 70–71
editing xi, 10, 18, 22–23, 28, 30–31,
   40, 44, 49, 62, 64–66, 76–80,
   87, 111, 118
engagement 109–113, 124, 130
envelope 40–41
episode 3–4, 8–9, 18, 21, 23, 34, 37,
   39, 43–44, 46–52, 62, 78–82,
   85, 89, 91, 94–98, 100, 105,
   107, 118–119, 123, 132–139,
   145, 156, 160, 170, 180–183
EQ 42, 69, 83–84, 88
excessive reverberation 70
exclusivity 170
export 63, 89–92
external recorder 55–56

F

Facebook 3, 48, 100–101, 106–107,
   109–113, 119–120, 124–125
feedback 10, 22, 38, 44–45, 50–51,
   74–75, 109, 119, 136
file management 78
file naming 91
first episode x, 18, 37, 46–50, 156
Fiverr 101–102
Fletcher-Munson curve 41
Flynn, Pat 143

focus 24, 38–39, 46, 51, 55, 60, 63, 73, 76, 86, 106, 110, 114, 122, 135, 139, 150, 156, 182
format 3, 25, 89, 112, 153
forum 102
freelance 101
    freelancer 30, 101
    Freelancer (platform) 102
frequency 21, 40–42, 54, 56–58, 60, 68, 70, 74, 83
    frequency range 42, 54, 60
    frequency response 54
FTP 95–97

G

GarageBand 63, 78
geo-targeting 96, 138
Google 25, 31, 45, 49, 94, 97, 105–106, 110, 112, 121, 124, 141, 150
    Play Music 105
ground work 78

H

Hall, Timothy 8
harmonic content 40
headphones 21, 41, 52, 59–62, 65, 70, 74, 86–88, 180
hosting 9, 18, 38, 47, 50, 90–91, 93–99, 105, 133–134, 137–138, 170, 175, 180
Howl 138, 161

I

influencer marketing 124–125, 144
influencers 124–125, 132–133

Instagram 31, 106–107, 110–111, 120, 124, 132
instrument 21, 57, 59, 82
internet 3, 9–12, 17, 20, 23, 34, 44, 64, 101, 110, 113, 116, 118, 124, 131–132, 143–146, 149, 178–179
iTunes 4, 9, 25, 27, 31–35, 48–49, 92, 94, 98, 100–106, 123, 166
    feature 100, 104, 106
Izotope Rx 78, 80

K

Keller, Gary W. 38
Kelly, Kevin 112, 156
keyword planner 49
Kickstarter 155, 158–159

L

lead 52, 141, 173, 181
legal 19, 35, 167, 174–176, 180
Libsyn 97, 138, 162
limited liability company 174
LinkedIn 110
Logic 63
logo 34, 100–107, 146, 149
Lore 105
loudness 40–42, 88
loudspeakers 60–61, 71, 74, 86

M

MailChimp 114
Making a Murderer 7, 117
marketing xi, 10, 17–18, 23–24, 27, 32, 39, 48, 50, 112, 114,

116–118, 120, 124–125, 129,
   132, 135, 136, 141, 143–146,
   152, 179
internet 17, 23
mastering 62, 76, 84, 87–90
merchandise 18, 148–149, 151–153,
   155, 157, 160, 168, 173, 179
Merchify 151
metadata 35, 91–92, 100, 107
microphone 9, 40, 50, 52–60,
   64–75, 158, 179
   condenser 53–54, 59, 65, 67–68
   dynamic 53–54, 57, 65, 67–68, 88
   USB microphone 55–60, 65
Midroll 138, 161
mixing xi, 28, 31, 41–42, 47, 54,
   61–62, 71, 76–77, 82–87, 180
monetising 18, 24, 160
money x, 6, 10, 18, 23, 26, 28, 36, 50,
   59, 64–65, 71, 101–102,
   114, 116, 122–124, 129–140,
   143–146, 149, 154, 155–160
mono 84, 88–90
motivation 28, 36
MP3 87, 90–92
music ix, 4, 7–10, 20, 28–31, 39,
   43–44, 59–63, 78–90, 112,
   131, 148
Musical.ly 110
MyLibsyn 161
MySpace 110

N

name 4, 8, 23, 26, 34, 47–49, 92,
   98, 103–104, 107, 137
newsletter 37, 109, 111–114, 123, 139,
   144–146
niche 22, 31–32, 130, 160

O

offers xi, 19, 20, 89, 114, 122, 131,
   136, 168–173
outro 43, 44, 76
outsourcing 101, 103

P

panning 83
Papasan, Jay 38
Patreon 107, 112, 154, 156–159
PayPal Button 158
pay-to-play 160, 162
paywall 160–162, 172
pencil technique 69
People Per Hour 102
physical products 146
Pinterest 110
PodBean 98
podcast x–xi, 3–12, 17–37, 39–40,
   43–56, 60–65, 76–84, 87–92,
   101–105, 117–125, 143–146
   advertisement 133
podcasting x–xi, 3–12, 17–37, 39–40,
   43–56, 60–65, 76–84,
   87–92, 101–105, 117–125,
   143–146
   apps 48, 94, 98, 104
polar pattern 55
   bidirectional 55
   cardioid 55
   omnidirectional 55
   unidirectional 55
pop shield 62, 65
premium content 96, 160, 172
Printify 151
production x–xi, 4, 9–13, 18, 25,
   29–31, 39, 44, 46, 49–50,

60–64, 67, 76, 111, 118–119, 143, 160–162, 169–170, 181
post-production 18, 44, 49, 63–64, 67, 69, 76, 87, 160
pre-production 76
profits 132, 179
Pro Tools 63–65, 80, 85, 89
  Pro Tools First 63, 65
proximity effect 67–68
publishing 23, 170

R

radio 3, 20–21, 133, 183
recording x, 7, 9, 18, 23, 38–40, 43–44, 49–56, 59–64, 67–75, 76–80, 175
  basics 67–75
  equipment x, 38, 43, 52–66, 175
RedBubble 149–150, 153
Reddit 102, 110, 120
reflection shield 62, 65
requirements 34, 104–105
research 7–9, 27–28, 30–33, 46–50, 64, 110, 131–133
responsibility 155, 167, 178–181
reverb 70, 83
ROI 124, 135, 159
Rogan, Joe 7, 166
royalty free 81
RSS 94–99, 100, 103
RT60 70

S

sales commission 143–144
Serial 7, 117, 183
sibilance 69

Snapchat 110–111
social media 4, 18, 26, 32, 106, 109–113, 145–146
software 52, 60, 62–66, 77, 82, 91, 110, 143, 146
sound x, 4–5, 9–10, 21–23, 28–31, 34, 40–48, 51, 53–74, 76–90
  card 59
  editor 22, 78–79
SoundCloud 94–95, 97
speakers 52, 60–61, 71, 74, 86
speed 41, 73, 77, 83, 122
SPL 41–42
sponsored post 116, 124
sponsorship 122, 131–141
Spotify 99
Spreadshirt 149–150
Squarespace 113
stability 77
standing waves 70
statistics 20, 25, 95–98, 134, 162
stereo 55, 59, 84–85, 88–90
Stitcher 98, 138, 161
  Premium 161
studio monitors 60–61
subscription 64, 104, 123, 158, 161
surround 59
Sunstein, Cass R. 132

T

Teespring 152
Thaler, Richard, H. 132
theme 9, 44, 81–83, 89, 111, 113
traffic 93, 110, 113–114, 121, 124, 139
Tumblr 110
TV 20, 103, 132–135, 169, 176, 179
  deal 169

Twitch 31
Twitter 31, 100, 106–107, 110–111

U

unbalanced frequencies 70
Upwork 101–102

V

velocity 40
virality 117–118
voice   i, 4, 7–8, 21, 42–44,
        52–54, 56, 67–69, 71–73, 77,
        83–84, 88–99, 101, 133, 173
volume 67, 83–88, 150

W

waveform 40
wavelength 40–41
website ix, 31–32, 36, 49–50, 94–95,
        98, 100, 105, 107, 109,
        113–114, 121, 141, 144–145, 158
Welles, Orson 3, 20
Wix 113

Y

YouTube 17, 20, 23, 43, 51, 60, 106,
        110, 121, 124–125, 132, 146

Z

Zazzle 149–150

Printed in Great Britain
by Amazon